Your 10-Day Spiritual Action Plan for

OVERCOMING
Stress, Anxiety
&Depression

KENNETH
COPELAND
PUBLICATIONS

by Kenneth and Gloria Copeland

Unless otherwise noted, all scripture is from the *King James Version* of the Bible.

Scripture quotations marked *The Amplified Bible* are from *The Amplified Bible, Old Testament* © 1965, 1987 by the Zondervan Corporation. *The Amplified New Testament* © 1958, 1987 by The Lockman Foundation. Used by permission.

Scripture quotations marked *New King James Version* are from the *New King James Version* © 1982 by Thomas Nelson Inc.

Scripture quotations marked *New International Version* are from *The Holy Bible, New International Version* © 1973, 1978, 1984 by the International Bible Society. Used by permission of Zondervan Publishing House.

Scripture quotations marked *New Living Translation* are from the Holy Bible, *New Living Translation* © 1996, 2004 by Tyndale Charitable Trust. Used by permission of Tyndale House Publishers.

Scripture quotations marked *Weymouth* are from *The New Testament in Modern Speech* by Richard Francis Weymouth © 1996 Kenneth Copeland Publications.

Includes material from the *Believer's Voice of Victory* magazine, *Freedom From Fear, God's Will Is Prosperity, Are You Listening?, Sorrow Not!, In Love There Is No Fear, To Know Him,* Kenneth Copeland's Partner Letters, as well as newly created content and interactive action plans inspired by these resources.

Your 10-Day Spiritual Action Plan for Overcoming Stress, Anxiety and Depression

ISBN 978-1-60463-291-0   30-3050

20 19 18 17 16 15   6 5 4 3 2 1

© 2015 Eagle Mountain International Church Inc. aka Kenneth Copeland Ministries

For more information about Kenneth Copeland Ministries, visit kcm.org or call 1-800-600-7395 (U.S. only) or +1-817-852-6000.

CD Credits:

Executive Producers: Kenneth and Gloria Copeland
Produced and Engineered by: Win Kutz
Production Assistant: Len Mink | Assistant Engineers: Leland Bennett, Michael Howell
Arranged by: Jerry Cleveland | Keyboards: Jerry Cleveland | Percussion: Jim DeLong
Lead Vocal: Len Mink | Background Vocalists: Paul Smith, Don Wallace, Karen Cruse Adams, Michael
Howell | Additional Vocals: KCM Choir
Scripture Readings by: Kenneth and Gloria Copeland

Recorded and Mixed at: Eagle Mountain Recording Studio, Newark, Texas
Mastered by: Allan Yoshida, The Mastering Lab, Hollywood, Calif.
Re-Mastered by: Michael Howell at Legendary Sound Studio, Fort Worth, TX

Wonderful Peace

W.G. Cooper
Public Domain
Scripture Reference: Philippians 4:4-7

Turn Your Eyes Upon Jesus

Helen H. Lemmel
Public Domain

Jesus, Name Above All Names

Naida Hearn
© 1974 Universal Music/Brentwood Benson Publ. (ASCAP) (admin. at CapitolCMGPublishing.com) All
rights reserved. Used by permission.
Scripture References: Psalms 23:1-6, 46:1, 50:15, 27:5, 107:28-30, 139:17

You Are My Hiding Place

Michael Ledner
© 1993 CCCM Music (ASCAP) Universal Music/Brentwood Benson Publ. (ASCAP) (admin. at CapitolC-
MGPublishing.com) All rights reserved. Used by permission.
Scripture References: Psalm 91; Isaiah 53:4-5

Be Still My Soul

Katharina von Schlegel (Trans. by Jane L. Borthwick), Jean Sibelius
Public Domain
Scripture References: Proverbs 3:5-6; Psalm 119:105; Matthew 11:28-29

My Peace

Keith Routledge
© 1975 Sovereign Music UK (PRS) (admin. at CapitolCMGPublishing.com) All rights reserved. Used by
permission.
Scripture References: Colossians 2:9; 1 John 4:13; Hebrews 4:16; Ephesians 3:20; Colossians 3:15-16;
Psalm 34:7; Isaiah 40:4; Hebrews 13:5; 2 Chronicles 20:15

He Is Our Peace

Kandela Groves

© 1987 CCCM Music (ASCAP) Universal Music /Brentwood Benson Publ. (ASCAP) (admin. at CapitolC-MGPublishing.com) All rights reserved. Used by permission.
Scripture References: Psalm 55:22; 1 Peter 5:7; Psalms 18:6, 118:5; 1 Kings 1:29; Psalm 107:28

Where the Spirit of the Lord Is

Steve Adams

© 1973 Pilot Point Music (Admin by Music Services)
Scripture Reference: Galatians 2:20

Near to the Heart of God

Cleland B. McAfee

Public Domain
Scripture References: Psalm 9:10; Hebrews 13:5; Matthew 28:20; 2 Corinthians 4:9; Romans 8:38-39

'Tis So Sweet to Trust in Jesus

Louisa M.R. Stead, William J. Kirkpatrick

Public Domain
Scripture Reference: Isaiah 26:3-4

Table of

Contents

Quick-Start Guide

LifeLine
Practical Tools for Everyday Needs

To start overcoming stress, anxiety and depression *now,* follow this **Quick-Start Guide...**

If you picked up this LifeLine Kit, then you already know the dangers and traps of living with stress, anxiety and/or depression. The good news is that you don't have to continue to live there. You can live in peace and confidence in God's love and provision for you. You can live without stress, anxiety, worry, panic, depression, fear, confusion—or anything else that would cause mental or emotional pain.

Commit to working through *Your 10-Day Spiritual Action Plan for Overcoming Stress, Anxiety and Depression* LifeLine Kit. Do it as though your life depended on it—because, in reality, it does! Your life of peace, joy, fulfillment, happiness and purpose depends on breaking the tentacles of stress, anxiety and/or depression.

If you're a born-again believer, inside you, already, is all the faith you need to produce the same results Jesus did (John 14:12)!

Understand that you are beginning a journey toward freedom. And, if you'll put the lessons in this package into practice, you'll receive the freedom God has for you. If you need to jump-start your journey, then begin implementing the steps in this quick-start guide. Let it be a starting point as you work through this study in greater depth.

1. Recognize that you are in a fight against fear.

You're not merely trying to *control* stress, anxiety and depression. You're in an all-out attack against them, and ultimately, against fear—fear that whatever situations you face are bigger than you can handle. But the God you serve is more than enough to defeat those attacks and help you adjust your focus.

2. Give The WORD of God first place.

In Joshua 1:7-8, The LORD tells Joshua to meditate on the book of the Law (His WORD) day and night. Like him, your victory over stress, anxiety and/or depression depends on giving God's WORD first place. Ponder what it says, pray it out loud, proclaim it and practice it. Immerse yourself in it. The *zoe* life of God that fills His WORD will flood your being and begin driving out fear—stress, anxiety and/or depression—so you can enjoy the rest and freedom you seek. (You can start with the scriptures on the Faith in Action cards in this book!)

3. Pray.

You need the guidance and wisdom of the Holy Spirit to adjust your thinking so, along with The WORD, you can follow His guidance to be free from stress, anxiety and/or depression. You'll need to get serious about spending time in prayer so you can connect with God—the Source of your peace.

First Thessalonians 5:17 tells you to pray without ceasing. Jude 20 says to pray in the Holy Ghost. And, be sure to include time to get quiet before The LORD so you can hear what He is speaking to you.

4. Decide to live by faith.

Let the time you spend thinking about and pondering what God says in His WORD and praying, change the way you perceive your environment. Understand that you are *not* a victim without hope. You are a child of God, and the price has already been paid for your freedom.

5. Commit to walk in love.

Galatians 5:6 explains the vital connection between faith and love. It tells you that faith works by love. So give your faith walk a boost by forgiving those who have wronged you. The power of forgiveness and the power of healing are the same. Love others with the grace that your heavenly Father extends to you. His healing power will flow. And, let the fruit of the spirit operate in your life (Galatians 5:22-23).

Put these steps into practice as you work through *Your 10-Day Spiritual Action Plan.* Embrace the change in thinking and attitude you are welcoming into your life. Allow the Holy Spirit to rewrite the way you process your surroundings so you can live free from stress, anxiety and/or depression. You're on your way!

Your Quick-Start Prayer

Father, thank You that You have led me to this moment of change. I submit my whole being to You—spirit, soul and body. As I begin this journey toward freedom from stress, anxiety and/or depression, I pray You'll direct and lead me by Your Holy Spirit. I commit to putting these faith steps into practice, to look to You, Your Holy Spirit and Your WORD for guidance. I trust You will meet all my needs according to Your riches in glory. I trust what You said in Your WORD and proclaim that by the stripes of Jesus, I am healed. I speak to the mountain of (insert name of mountain here) _____ to be removed and cast into the sea!

Thank You that Your WORD is true. I know that I can trust You, and that Your love surrounds me and lifts me up to receive all You have for me.

In the Name of Jesus. Amen!

Your Promises From God's WORD

- Romans 8:2
- John 16:33
- Isaiah 26:3
- Isaiah 53:4-5
- 1 John 4:18
- Psalm 91:1-7

You will find more prayers, confessions and scriptures listed in the back of this book.

How to Use
Your LifeLine Kit

How to Use
Your LifeLine Kit

We believe *Your 10-Day Spiritual Action Plan for Overcoming Stress, Anxiety and Depression* will give you the tools you need to fulfill God's plan for your life and enjoy a life of freedom, joy and peace.

To accomplish this, we've created one of the most in-depth resources with step-by-step guidance, that Kenneth Copeland Ministries has ever made available on this subject—all in one place!

Here are some practical tips to get you started and help you make the most of this kit:

- Commit to making the next 10 days *your* days for renewing your mind. Set aside any distractions and be prepared to make adjustments in your life so you can get the most out of this kit.

- This plan should be a blessing, not a burden. If you miss a day or can't quite get through one day's materials, simply start where you left off at your next opportunity. If you have to, be flexible with the kit to ensure you make it to the end. If you only have half an hour a day, that's fine—commit that! It may take longer to complete the kit, but you can be confident those days will still be some of the most life-changing you've ever experienced.

- Use this LifeLine workbook as your starting point each day, to guide your reading, listening, watching and journaling. Before you know it, your life will be saturated with God's WORD like never before.

- We recommend that you:

  > ▶ **Read and journal** in the morning
  >
  > ▶ **Meditate** on the scriptures daily
  >
  > ▶ **Use** the CD and DVD products daily as instructed in each chapter
  >
  > ▶ **Read and journal** again at night

- Remember, the goal is to do a little every day. Steady doses are the best medicine.

- This is an action book! Have a pen handy to underline and take notes.

- Fully engage with all the materials. Write in your workbook, speak the scriptures, pray the prayers, sing with the music and take time to enjoy the materials in every way.

- Carry your daily action card and refer to it throughout your day as a point of connection with God.

- Make your study time focused. Do your best to remove distractions and find a quiet place.

You are closer than ever to putting stress, anxiety and/or depression far behind you. And always remember that God loves you and He is *for* you. We're standing with you, and remember, "Jesus Is LORD!"

Chapter One
The War on Fear

The Life God Designed for You
by Kenneth Copeland

Gloria and I are thrilled you've decided to work through this LifeLine Kit! So many accept stress, anxiety and/or depression as a normal part of life. Without knowing how to walk free of these killers, they try to manage them, living with them day in, and day out. But, I want to share with you what The LORD has shown me. Stress, anxiety and/or depression, and all that goes with them, stem from the same root—fear.

And fear has no place in the life of any believer.

On Oct. 18, 2001, in a hotel in Washington, D.C., The LORD began talking to me about Kenneth Copeland Ministries' place and commission—its role and anointing. I realized He was talking to me about the very reason I was born, the reason I was put into this ministry and the reason for my own personal calling.

All the things God has been so gracious to allow me to see, all the things He has called me to do and all the things I've been privileged to learn about His WORD came to this defining moment. The LORD told me to take this ministry into an all-out attack against the spirit of fear....He said, *Pull the plug on terrorism!*

Take a look around. Almost all you see and hear these days is *fear*. It's everywhere, whether it's cloaked as stress, anxiety and/or depression or panic.

But it's not so surprising—that's what *terror*-ism is all about.

Terrorism is defined as "the planned, organized use of fear as a weapon." The goal of terrorism is to terrify, frighten or panic to the point that a person or people cannot resist.

Oppression Is the spoiling or taking away of a person's goods or estates by terror or force. It means taking them away without having any right to them, and by working on the ignorance, weakness or *fearfulness* of the person being oppressed.

At the heart of all terrorism and oppression is fear. But, unlike the rest of the world, believers don't have to cope with or tolerate fear and its many forms in any way. We attack it and get rid of it. Think about that: *You* can attack and get rid of fear, stress, anxiety and/or depression. No longer do you have to give it any place in your life. You can be free!

There's a huge difference between just coping with fear and its byproducts, trying to "make it" through life while still subject to all fear's oppression, and being totally delivered—where fear is completely out of your life, forever.

As a born-again child of God, you don't have to settle for being dominated or controlled by fear anymore because Jesus destroyed the *root* of all fear. In other words, because of Jesus' sacrifice on the cross, you no longer have a spirit of fear living *inside* you, and as a result, you can be free from stress, anxiety and/or depression. Let your journey begin!

Morning
Reflection

In your own words, define *fear.*

_____

_____

_____

How has fear impacted your life? Has it manifested as stress, anxiety and/or depression or some other way? Explain.

_____

_____

_____

According to Romans 8:2, "The law of the Spirit of life in Christ Jesus hath made [us] free from the law of sin and death." What kind of freedom are you believing for through this study?

_____

_____

_____

Today's
Connection Points

- ### *Selections From Peaceful Praise* CD: "Wonderful Peace" (Track 1)

  Allow God's glorious peace to rule in your heart today as you listen to the music and rest in His presence.

- ### DVD: "Dwelling in Your Safe Place" (Chapter 1)

  The secret place of the Most High is your place of refuge and peace. Experience His rest when you dwell under the shadow of His wings.

- ### Scriptures CD (Track 1)

  2 Timothy 1:7; John 17:20-23; 1 John 4:15-18; Isaiah 43:1-3; Deuteronomy 31:6; Psalm 91

Faith in Action

Determine to focus on God's peace today, regardless of what's happening around you.

When stress, anxiety and/or depression tries to fasten its grip on you, begin to thank and praise God for His great love for you and the sacrifice He made on Calvary so you could be free.

Put It Into Practice

You Are Not Alone!

If you are reading this LifeLine Kit and thinking that you are alone, be encouraged—you are not! Stress, anxiety and/or depression affect millions of people worldwide, and the results are far-reaching. Just look at these staggering statistics:

- One in four Canadian workers admits to feeling highly stressed in their daily lives.[1]
- Annually, about 12 million people in the U.K. visit their general practitioners for mental illness treatment, ranging from anxiety to depression.[2]
- As many as 40 million Americans suffer from an anxiety disorder.[3]
- Government officials in Australia anticipate that 45 percent of their citizens will struggle with a mental health issue—most likely depression or anxiety—at some point in their lives.[4]
- The World Health Organization estimates that more than 350 million people worldwide suffer from depression, and that it is the most common reason for disability.[5]

Stress is a leading factor in the development of depression, anxiety and panic disorders. Common symptoms of stress include headaches, chest pain, muscle pain, upset stomach, insomnia, irritability, sadness, overeating, substance abuse, fatigue and social withdrawal.[6] If you struggle with any of these symptoms or have even received a confirmed diagnosis,

1 "What's Stressing the Stressed?," Susan Compton, *Canada Statistics,* http://www.statcan.gc.ca/pub/11-008-x/2011002/article/11562-eng.htm (5/12/2015).
2 "Stress," *Mental Health Foundation,* http://www.mentalhealth.org.uk/help-information/mental-health-a-z/S/stress (5/12/2015).
3 "Facts and Statistics," *Anxiety and Depression Organization of America,* http://www.adaa.org/about-adaa/press-room/facts-statistics (5/12/2015).
4 "Depression, Anxiety," *beyondblue,* http://www.beyondblue.org.au/the-facts (5/12/2015).
5 "Depression Fact Sheet, No. 369, Oct. 2012," *World Health Organization Media Center,* http://www.who.int/mediacentre/factsheets/fs369/en (5/12/2015).
6 "Healthy Lifestyle Stress Management," Mayo Clinic Staff, *Mayo Clinic,* http://www.mayoclinic.org/healthy-living/stress-management/in-depth/stress-symptoms/art-20050987 (5/12/2015).

then by reading—and implementing—the teaching in this LifeLine Kit, you are taking positive steps toward your healing. Jesus said, "I am come that they might have life… and have it more abundantly" (John 10:10).

Let this *Spiritual Action Plan* begin the start of a new life, free from stress, anxiety and/or depression and any other challenge the devil tries to throw your way. And, if you need someone to agree in prayer with you, or would like to order more teaching materials that will help you further, contact the KCM office nearest you. We love you and are here to help!

Notes:

Where There's Safety, Security and Peace

by Gloria Copeland

What Ken shared with you this morning is so true: Fear is everywhere. The closer and closer we get to the end of this age, the more dangerous and difficult things become and, as a result, the temptation to give in to stress, anxiety and/or depression becomes very real. The Bible warned us it would be this way.

Second Timothy 3:1-3 says:

> But understand this, that in the last days will come (set in) perilous times of great stress and trouble [hard to deal with and hard to bear]. For people will be lovers of self and [utterly] self-centered, lovers of money and aroused by an inordinate [greedy] desire for wealth, proud and arrogant and contemptuous boasters. They will be abusive (blasphemous, scoffing), disobedient to parents, ungrateful, unholy and profane. [They will be] without natural [human] affection (callous and inhuman), relentless (admitting of no truce or appeasement); [they will be] slanderers (false accusers, troublemakers), intemperate and loose in morals and conduct, uncontrolled and fierce, haters of good *(The Amplified Bible)*.

Those verses clearly describe the days we're living in. People in the world who have rejected the influence of God are charging after darkness and sin as fast as they can. It's apparent in their behavior, attitudes and even their dress.

"Oh, my," you might say, "that's bad news."

Not necessarily. There are two groups of people: the sinners who are headed for destruction and the members of God's family who have the promise of deliverance. The future of the sinner is extremely dark and sad, but the future of God's family is very bright and full of joy.

Isaiah 3:10-11 puts it this way. "Say to the righteous that it shall be well with them, for they shall eat the fruit of their doings. Woe to the wicked! It shall be ill with him, for the reward of his hands shall be given him" *(New King James Version)*.

God has invited everyone to become part of His family. He created man with a free will, allowing every person to choose whether he wants to walk in the light or the darkness. But if God had His heart's desire, every person would accept His invitation, become part of His family and walk in the light. The Bible tells us, "[God] is long-suffering (extraordinarily patient) toward you, not desiring that any should perish, but that all should turn to repentance" (2 Peter 3:9, *The Amplified Bible*).

All you have to do to get into God's family is recognize that you're a sinner, repent of your sin and make Jesus Christ The LORD of your life. Jesus came to earth and shed His blood so we could obtain forgiveness. If you haven't yet prayed to receive Him as your Savior and LORD, do it now. Turn to the back of this book and pray the prayer to make Jesus The LORD of your life. Or, call KCM's prayer line to talk with one of our prayer ministers. Don't wait another second to join God's family! We love you, and want you to experience the peace and joy of knowing Jesus as your Savior and LORD.

Once you're part of God's family, His promises of protection and deliverance are yours. You can live in security and safety, not just when you get to heaven in the sweet by-and-by, but right here on earth in the dangerous here-and-now!

Psalm 3:8 says, "Salvation belongs to The LORD. Your blessing is upon Your people" *(New King James Version)*. The New Testament echoes that truth in 1Thessalonians 5:9 and assures us that "God did not appoint us to wrath, but to obtain salvation through our LORD Jesus Christ" *(New King James Version)*.

The Greek word *soteria,* translated "salvation" in this scripture, means "wholeness, preservation, material and temporal deliverance from danger and apprehension, pardon, restoration, healing and soundness."[7]

God promises to provide these things for us as His children, even in dangerous or uncertain times. But obedience is key. Psalm 91 states that protection is available to those who obey The LORD: "He who dwells in the secret place of the Most High shall abide under the shadow of the Almighty. I will say of The LORD, 'He is my refuge and my fortress; my God, in Him I will trust.' Surely He shall deliver you from the snare of the fowler and from the perilous pestilence" (verses 1-3, *New King James Version*).

It is the person who abides in The LORD who enjoys supernatural safety in times of trouble. Day after day, in bad times and good, the abider stays fixed in his faith and obedience to God. This person is not out doing his own thing. He's running his life according to what God says is right. There's protection in that because God's ways work!

Over the next 10 days, keep this in mind. By just picking up this LifeLine Kit, you have taken the first step toward overcoming fear, stress, anxiety and/or depression. Continue to learn what The WORD has to say about the obstacles you face and your reaction to them, and then do what it says. As you do, you'll not just learn to manage stress, anxiety and/or depression, but you'll *eliminate* them, and rest knowing that you are safe, secure and at peace in all God has for you!

---

7 "Salvation," *Vine's Expository Dictionary of Biblical Words,* W.E. Vine, Merril F. Unger, William White (Nashville: Thomas Nelson Publishers, 1985) p. 545.

Evening Reflection

How would a better understanding of God's protection affect your peace of mind?

_____

_____

_____

Name the situations in your life in which you need the assurance of God's protection.

_____

_____

_____

How can you begin to abide in God's WORD...especially regarding the above situations? List 3-5 steps you can take in order to _abide_ in God's WORD.

_____

_____

_____

Today's Prayer of Faith

Father God, I commit to abide in You. Help me to walk in constant communication with You through Your WORD and prayer. I will put my trust and faith in You and trust You to guard me—spirit, soul and body. In Jesus' Name. Amen.

Real-Life Testimonies
to Help Build Your Faith

My Mind Renewed, and Free From Fear!

I thank God for you and your ministry! As I was watching Kenneth and Rick Renner, I was set free from fear and a lot of other things that were troubling me.

From January 2012, I experienced a great, uncontrollable fear that came up in my belly, and at the same time, my shoulders would become heavy and my neck would get tight. At first, the fear would affect my heart, and it would palpitate. I went to the doctor more than once, and he would tell me everything was fine. At night, I could not sleep because of the fear, and then I began to tell myself I would die in my sleep.

Thank God for His WORD! As I listened to Kenneth and Rick, I soaked up The WORD and received it, and my mind was renewed. I am free from all that fear and the lies of the enemy. Praise and thanks be unto God who gives me the victory, in Jesus' Name—hallelujah! Continue to preach The WORD!

Hyacinth D.
Canada

Chapter Two
Faith—The Opposite of Fear

Identifying Counterfeits
by Kenneth Copeland

Yesterday, I began talking to you about the root of stress, anxiety and/or depression, which is fear. And, fear is the work of the enemy from whom we have been delivered.

Today, I want to continue to expose how Satan uses fear to control and dominate. Even believers can be terrorized by fear and all that comes with it, namely stress, anxiety and/or depression. However, freedom from this terror was purchased on the Cross. Jesus paid the price for it, and we can live free from fear.

Romans 8:2 says, "For the law of the Spirit of life in Christ Jesus hath made me free from the law of sin and death."

This verse of scripture sets out the two basic spiritual laws at work in the world: *the law of the Spirit of life* (in Christ Jesus) and *the law of sin and death* (in Satan). Webster's dictionary defines a *law* as "an established principle." You can depend on a law to work the same way every time.

The two laws in Romans 8:2 are reciprocals. The word *reciprocal* means "corresponding, but reversed or inverted." Let me give you an illustration of this: North and south are reciprocals. They correspond to one another because they are both directions on a compass, but south is the reciprocal of north. They are exact opposites of each other.

Understanding the principle of reciprocals gives insight into how Satan operates. Satan is a fallen angel. Like all angelic beings, he has no creative power. He cannot create; he can only destroy. He can only work with the things already created. He is limited to the forces in this world. Had he ever come up with anything original, that thing would be a truth. But Jesus said there is no truth in him (John 8:44). He is a counterfeiter, a deceiver.

Satan became the illegitimate stepfather of mankind through Adam's high treason in the Garden of Eden. He received Adam's authority over the spiritual laws in the earth. He did not put spiritual law into motion. He just perverted the laws that were already there.

- Sin was righteousness perverted
- Death was life perverted
- Hate was love perverted
- Fear was faith perverted.

The faith that God gave Adam was meant to sustain his life. When Satan gained control, that force of faith was perverted. Satan then used that perverted spiritual force of fear to steal, kill and destroy.

After Adam sinned in the Garden, fear became the dominant force in his life. The first words he spoke to God were, "I was afraid" (Genesis 3:10). The faith he had in his heart was turned into fear. This is why faith and fear are so closely related. They are almost identical. They work the same way, but produce opposite results.

The law of reciprocals works in every area. God's WORD is true, but there is no truth in Satan. Satan counterfeits God in every situation. And, since stress, anxiety, panic and/or depression are closely related to fear, they, too, are counterfeits of faith. Remember, the counterfeit is *never* as powerful as the real thing.

There is a promise in God's WORD that will overcome every opportunity to fail that Satan can throw our way. There is not one thing in Satan's bag of tricks that The WORD cannot overcome. By knowing the spiritual law of reciprocals and how it operates, we can keep Satan out of our lives.

That's good news because as we take our stand against stress, anxiety and/or depression—and every other fear symptom—we can stand in faith, knowing that they can be defeated and driven out of our lives.

This week, as you go about your business, stop to identify any counterfeits. When you begin to feel the effects of stress, anxiety and/or depression, stop and declare that you walk according to the law of the Spirit of life in Christ Jesus. Commit to do this as you interact with your spouse or family members, when you deal with financial struggles, when you encounter conflict with family, friends or a co-worker, or when you stand for healing from an illness or injury.

Fear, stress, anxiety and/or depression are not God's will for your life. Recognize them for what they are—counterfeits—and begin to gain the victory over them with The WORD and prayer! In the Evening Connection, you'll learn more about how to do just that.

Morning Reflection

What counterfeits have been part of your life—anger, fear, stress, anxiety, panic, depression? List them and the opposite, or reciprocal, of each one.

_____

_____

_____

Now that you have a better understanding of the law of reciprocals, how can you change the way you respond to the counterfeits when they arise?

_____

_____

_____

List two scriptures on which you will stand this week for your peace of mind.

_____

_____

_____

Today's
Connection Points

- **Selections From Peaceful Praise CD: "Turn Your Eyes Upon Jesus" (Track 2)**

  When you look at the Savior, there's no room for anything else! Stress, anxiety and/or depression melt away in the presence of the Prince of Peace.

- **DVD: "The Anointing to Remove Fear" (Chapter 2)**

  The Anointed One and His Anointing of love dwells mightily in you, driving out all fear and destroying every yoke of bondage.

- **Scriptures CD (Track 2)**

  Hebrews 11:1-6; Romans 8:2, 31-32, 35-39; Isaiah 26:3; Deuteronomy 7:9; Psalm 89:1; Romans 4:16, 5:1-2, 8:15

Faith
in Action

Confess this personalized scripture over yourself today:

"For the law of the Spirit of life in Christ Jesus hath made me, [Insert your name here], free from the law of sin and death."

Put It Into Practice

Here and Now

Regrets from the past. Concerns for the future. Enduring a mental barrage of what you *should* be doing. Is that where you live? Are you so consumed with what has happened or might happen that you can't enjoy what is happening right now?

Make the commitment to begin living in the present—not the past or the future. When distracting thoughts come to mind, take a stand and confess to The LORD, "You will keep me in perfect peace because my mind is stayed on You, and I trust in You" (Isaiah 26:3).

Other strategies to help you remain in the present include:

1. Resisting the urge to multi-task. Multi-tasking keeps your focus divided on too many things and actually reduces productivity.[8] Instead, give whatever you are doing your complete attention, and then move on to the next item on your to-do list.

2. Keep a prayer journal. When thoughts come to mind for which you need the leading of the Holy Spirit, write them in your prayer journal. Understand that worrying about them won't change the outcome—only prayer, wisdom and obedience to the Holy Spirit will. And don't forget to note when and how The LORD answers your prayers. Over time, you'll be encouraged by how The LORD has worked in your life.

3. Dig into the Scriptures. Let God's WORD change the way you think about your situation (Romans 12:2). When troublesome thoughts come to mind, speak those scriptures out loud. Pray them. Post them where you can see them throughout your day, and ask the Holy Spirit to reveal their meaning to you.

You don't have to live with the mental torment that comes from regretting yesterday and worrying about tomorrow. Put these strategies to work, and allow God's WORD to adjust your thinking so you can experience more peace throughout your day.

8 "Executive control of cognitive processes in task switching," Rubinstein JS, Meyer DE, Evans JE. *Journal of Experimental Psychology: Human Perception and Performance.* 2001; 27(4): 763-797, http://www.apa.org/pubs/journals/releases/xhp274763.pdf, (1-27-2015).; "Is Too Much Juggling Causing You Brain Drain?" Steve Sisgold, *Psychology Today,* Feb. 26, 2014, https://www.psychologytoday.com/blog/life-in-body/201402/is-too-much-juggling-causing-you-brain-drain (1/27/2015).

You Can Live Free!
by Kenneth Copeland

This morning, we learned about reciprocals, or spiritual opposites. This evening, let's continue with this, especially as it relates to fear and faith. Understanding this revelation is an important first step to freedom from stress, anxiety and/or depression.

The price Jesus paid on the cross was twofold. He came, to not only destroy the works of the devil (all the counterfeits we discussed this morning), but also to deliver us from the fear of death and its bondage. Look at Hebrews 2:14-15: "Forasmuch then as the children are partakers of flesh and blood, he also himself likewise took part of the same; that through death he might destroy him that had the power of death, that is, the devil; and deliver them who through fear of death were all their lifetime subject to bondage."

The phrase *fear of death* is a result of the law of sin and death. The word *destroy* in the original text means "to paralyze." So, Jesus came for two reasons:

1. To *completely paralyze* Satan who had the power of death
2. To *deliver* us who, through fear of death, were held subject to bondage

In order for the power of death to ever be broken, Jesus had to absorb all the curse of the law, both in the spiritual and physical realms. When the price was paid, God breathed the breath of life into Jesus, and the law of the Spirit of life was set into motion for mankind. Because He did all that for you and me, we can live free! We can know beyond doubt that the law of the Spirit of life in Christ Jesus has made *us* free from the law of sin and death!

When you were born again, your human spirit was completely re-created (Romans 8:15). You received all the qualities, spiritual forces and things of God resident in Adam when God created him in the Garden of Eden. Plus, you received all the things in Jesus when God raised Him from the dead!

Notice these words: "Ye have not received the spirit of bondage again to fear" (Romans 8:15). Fear is not a natural force to the born-again believer. It was natural to you before you were reborn. But, your spirit man was re-created, and eternal life erupted in your heart when you made Jesus The LORD of your life.

Understand, fear is a spiritual force just as faith is a spiritual force. When you apply faith and operate in it by keeping The WORD of God in your heart, the faith of God will flow through your body to keep it well and whole. When you apply fear and operate in it, the force of fear will work against you to make you sick or stressed or anxious or depressed. Fear works in the spirit world the same way faith does—but as a reciprocal force.

Fear is a satanic force that works against you at every opportunity. Faith is a creative force that God uses to build and uplift. Faith helps; fear hurts. Whenever faith is in operation, you will always benefit from it. Whenever fear is in operation, you will be subject to bondage and torment.

Satan knows that he cannot do anything to you apart or separate from fear, just as God cannot do anything for you apart or separate from faith. Satan can't touch you as long as you stand on The WORD of God.

Faith power is not produced in your head; it is produced in your heart. It is produced by The WORD of God being fed into your spirit. You will never get any power out of your car by pouring water into the gas tank. Your spirit life derives its power from God's WORD the way your car derives its power from gasoline. If you operate in fear and feed fear down into your spirit, you will never produce the kind of faith power it takes to rule over the stress, anxiety and/or depression of this life.

Instead, begin feeding on God's WORD. This morning you found two scriptures and began standing in faith on them by writing them, praying them and speaking them. That was the beginning of your faith journey. Continue to search God's WORD for scriptures on which to base your faith. Ask The LORD to lead you during your Bible study time. Let this be the beginning of your journey to freedom from stress, anxiety and/or depression. You're on your way!

Evening Reflection

Why are faith and fear opposites?

_____

_____

_____

How does faith overcome fear and stress, and how can you begin using faith to stand against stress, anxiety, worry and/or depression in your life?

_____

_____

_____

Where is faith produced and from where does your spirit man derive its power to overcome stress, anxiety and/or depression?

_____

_____

_____

Today's
Prayer of Faith

Father, thank You for allowing me to live in the law of the Spirit of life in Christ Jesus and adopting me into Your family. I ask that Your Holy Spirit would help me recognize any counterfeits that would try to distract me from living an overcoming life in Christ. In Jesus' Name. Amen.

Real-Life Testimonies
to Help Build Your Faith

We Refused to Fear

A few weeks ago, I asked your ministry to stand in faith with us for my husband, regarding his job. I wanted to let you know what has happened!

While sitting in his office, after he had finished every last piece of work he could do for anyone, my husband received a phone call from a job agency asking if he would be interested in a position that had just come through. He interviewed for the position and got the job! It pays almost twice as much as the previous job and he's working on developing a database doing exactly what he's wanted to do.

Praise God, He is so good! We are rejoicing and very thankful. Thank you for standing with us. We refused to give place to fear, and trusted God, thanking Him for my husband's next assignment and it came quickly! Thank you once again for teaching us the truth and how to trust God.

J.M.
U.K.

Notes:

Chapter Three
Exposing the Terrorist

Understanding the Enemy's Weapon
by Kenneth Copeland

On the first day of this study, I shared with you the mission The LORD gave this ministry—to pull the plug on terrorism. That mandate encompasses a lot of ground because fear has many faces. It can appear as outright fear and panic, or it can be more subtle and manifest as worry, anxiety and stress. Fear can paralyze a person to the point where they can't move or speak and can make a person physically sick.

In recent years, *controlling* fear has been a common topic. Sometimes, if we work at it hard enough, we can control specific fears in our natural strength. But it will always manifest in other ways, and merely controlling it in specific areas falls far short of the total victory Jesus won over death and all fear at the cross.

Let's clarify the difference between coping with fear and every symptom that comes with it, and totally *eradicating* the spirit of fear. For the purpose of illustration, let's use the example of a professional rodeo cowboy…a champion bull rider.

What this man does for a living is something the average spectator would consider very frightening. He gets on an animal that weighs thousands of pounds, and that bull is mad at everything that moves. Seconds later, he's trying to ride the thing with all kinds of opposition from the bull. And, when the cowboy's ride is over or he gets thrown off, the bull does his best to gore or stomp him.

Though it's very dangerous, the cowboy has trained himself and ridden enough that he is not afraid to get on that bull. Yet the same man, while driving to the next performance, can be worried sick about his finances, his family, his own life and everything around him.

Why? Because fear is still present. Through logic, training and using various mental techniques, he's learned to put down fear when riding a bull, but it still runs rampant in other areas of his life.

Now if that same cowboy locks into The WORD of God, discovers how to receive total deliverance from fear and begins to walk in it, it'll be an entirely different situation. He will respect the danger, but he won't be afraid of the bull because he'll know God and know how to walk free from fear in this and every other area of his life.

Now, keep in mind that the *fear of death* is the root of all fear. It's where stress, anxiety and/or depression begin. Let's look at some of the fears people have concerning death and the different ways a person can die. There are basically four ways a person can die: at the hand of another human being, by starvation, because of an accident, or from sickness and disease.

To understand how the devil would try to use one of these four basic fears to his advantage, imagine a man who beats another person to within an inch of death. Then, he picks up his victim, brushes him off and leaves.

A few days later, when the victim is just barely recovering, the attacker returns and asks, "How are you doing?" The dumbfounded victim doesn't know what to say. He's so afraid he can hardly move.

"I'll tell you what," the assailant continues, "for $100 a week I'll see to it nobody ever does you that way again." Still speechless, the battered victim is thinking: *Who else would do me that way?*

"You know, the same thing could happen to you at almost any time," the attacker threatens.

Notice the attacker constantly promotes fear of himself. Then, the victim begins reading between the lines: *He's the one who's going to come back and do it! Or maybe his thugs are going to come back and kill me.*

So what has the attacker done? He has used fear and terror to try to extort money. He took a basic fear—in this case, fear of death at the hands of another person—amplified that fear and used it as a weapon of oppression and terror to take what does not belong to him.

In the same way, a variety of worries can spring out of the basic fear of death by starvation. For example, the concern about not having enough money to buy food may lead to thinking: *I don't want to offend my boss because he's the one who gave me this job, and I have to work for him. Taking my Bible to work might offend him. If I offend him, he'll fire me, and I'll wind up without any income. Then I won't have any money. And, if I don't have money, I won't have enough to eat!*

Do you see how your mind will run away with you if you don't attack fear at its root? You'll see the same pattern develop with any of the fears we've mentioned.

One, right after another, the devil introduces every possible method of dying in order to paralyze people and keep fear on their minds all the time. This strategy is designed to make their witness as Christians ineffective. And pretty soon, if unchecked, he will have undermined their faith. Once that happens, his ultimate goal is possible—to get The WORD out that has been sown into the believer's heart:

> ...when affliction or persecution ariseth for The WORD's sake, immediately they are offended. And these are they which are sown among thorns; such as hear The WORD, and the cares of this world, and the deceitfulness of riches, and the lusts of other things entering in, choke The WORD, and it becometh unfruitful (Mark 4:17-19).

Affliction, persecution, the cares of this world, the deceitfulness of riches and the lusts of other things are all tools Satan uses for one purpose—to steal The WORD out of the heart of the person who has received it with gladness.

All five of these tools depend on fear to work. And, Satan himself is behind every one of them. But when we shine the full force of the light of God's WORD on his devices, and renew our minds and words to what God has said—we expose a defeated and weaponless enemy. Satan has already been defeated and stripped of the only real weapon he ever had—the power of death and the fear that power created.

Now, in the light of God's WORD, this weaponless foe is being exposed for who he truly is, and in the Evening Connection, you'll learn more about the divine protection afforded you through what Jesus did on the cross. Remember, Satan's No. 1 weapon is deception. All he can do is lie to you that God's WORD will not work for you. But if you won't believe him, he cannot stop The WORD from working in your life. And, if he cannot stop The WORD, he cannot stop you!

Morning Reflection

Describe how all stress, anxiety and/or depression is based in fear.

_____

_____

_____

Look at the five tools the enemy uses to induce fear. How has he used these tools against you?

_____

_____

_____

How is the stress, anxiety, panic and/or depression you face, based in a fear of death?

_____

_____

_____

Today's Connection Points

⊙ *Selections From Peaceful Praise* **CD: "Jesus, Name Above All Names" (Track 3)**

The Name of Jesus is above every fear and attack of the enemy. Sing His mighty Name today, and watch mountains move and demons flee.

⦿ **DVD: "Your Refuge in Him" (Chapter 3)**

He is your strong confidence and the rock of your refuge. Draw in to the strength of His love and the comfort of His peace.

⦿ **Scriptures CD (Track 3)**

John 10:10; Hebrews 2:14-15; James 4:7; Luke 10:19; Ephesians 6:10-17; Psalm 56:3; Isaiah 41:10

Faith in Action

When stressful or depressing thoughts come to your mind, stop and consider how they reflect a fear of death. Then, begin praising God that He has not given you a spirit of fear, but of love, power and a sound mind.
(2 Timothy 1:7)

Put It Into Practice

Feed Your Temple

God created you as a whole person—spirit, soul (mind, will and emotions) and body. And those three areas are interactive and impact each other. Your soul affects your body. And your body affects your soul, which in turn affects your spirit. As you work to build and strengthen your spirit, be sure to build and strengthen your body by feeding it the right foods. Here are five foods to include and five foods to remove from your diet to improve your health and mood.

Five Foods to Include[9]

1. Asparagus—The healthy dose of folic acid found in asparagus can help fight depression and boost your mood. Just one cup supplies two-thirds of your daily requirement of mood-boosting folic acid.
2. Avocado—This fruit is full of B vitamins, also known as stress vitamins for their abilities to lower stress reactions, improve mood and raise energy levels. Loaded with monosaturated fat and potassium, these "alligator pears" can also help lower blood pressure.

9 "13 Foods That Fight Stress," Keri Glassman, MS, RD, CDN, *Prevention,* http://www.prevention.com/mind-body/emotional-health/13-healthy-foods-reduce-stress-and-depression?s=5, (2/27/15); "Eat to Beat Stress: 10 Foods That Reduce Anxiety," Tanya Zuckerbrot, *Men's Fitness,* http://www.mensfitness.com/nutrition/what-to-eat/eat-to-beat-stress-10-foods-that-reduce-anxiety/slide/7 (5/12/2015).

3. Blueberries—These small berries pack a big punch of antioxidants and vitamin C, making them excellent stress fighters. Vitamin C has been shown to help fight high blood pressure and lower the stress hormone, cortisol.

4. Wild-caught salmon—Full of healthy omega-3s, this excellent protein source has been shown to decrease inflammation and keep cortisol and adrenaline levels from spiking, which means more peace in your body.

5. Cashews—These tasty nuts are high in zinc, a nutrient that is often deficient among those suffering from anxiety and depression.

Five Foods to Avoid[10]

1. Caffeine—Caffeine, which is found in coffee, tea, some sodas and many energy drinks, increases your heart rate, leading to increased feelings of anxiety, while lowering serotonin levels in your brain, which can lead to depression.

2. Sugar—Those sweet, white crystals can cause an imbalance in blood sugar, leading to quick initial energy followed by a crash that can leave you feeling tired and worn-out. Refined sugars are found in candy, white bread, pastries, white rice, pasta, cakes, crackers, chips and soft drinks, or sodas.

3. Wheat—Food allergies can often manifest in symptoms of anxiety or depression. One of the more common allergies is to foods containing gluten, a protein found in wheat, barley and rye.

4. Dairy—This is another well-known food allergy culprit that can cause feelings of anxiety and/or depression.

5. Salt—While flavorful, sodium chloride, or common table salt, can cause dehydration which is known to cause depression as well as lower potassium, a nutrient needed for a healthy nervous system.

First Corinthians 6:19-20 refers to your body as the temple of the Holy Spirit and encourages you to care for it properly. As you work through this *10-Day Spiritual Action Plan for Overcoming Stress, Anxiety and Depression* LifeLine Kit, commit to caring for your body and treating it with the respect it deserves. Feed it nourishing food, and avoid the processed, quick fix meals that can lead to unstable blood sugar levels, nervousness and fatigue. Let this study be the beginning of a whole new you—spirit, soul *and* body!

10 "Depression," *Food for the Brain: Championing Optimum Nutrition for the Mind,* http://www.foodforthebrain.org/nutrition-solutions/depression/about-depression.aspx, (1-28-2015); "Nine Foods That Help or Hurt Anxiety," Beth W. Orenstein, Anxiety Disorders, *Everyday Health,* http://www.everydayhealth.com/anxiety-pictures/anxiety-foods-that-help-foods-that-hurt-0118.aspx, (1-28-2015); "Foods That Cause Anxiety Attacks," R.Y. Langham, PhD., updated Nov. 13, 2010, *Livestrong.com,* http://www.livestrong.com/article/306192-foods-that-cause-anxiety-attacks (5/12/2015).

The Safety of God
by Gloria Copeland

*S*ecurity. That one word, perhaps more than any other, sums up what the world is searching for these days. Everyone wants to feel more secure—secure in their homes, secure in their jobs and secure in their relationships.

Is it possible to live in this crazy world with all its uncertainty and still feel secure? Yes, it is, and Psalm 91 tells us how.

I've loved and taught on this psalm for years. But I've never been more grateful for it than I am right now. It was definitely written for us today. If we will just believe and act on the words God spoke to us there, we will be able to live in total freedom from fear, stress, anxiety and/or depression and worry—even in the worst of times. No matter what kinds of stresses arise around us, we will be able to say to The LORD like David did, "What time I am afraid, I will trust in thee" (Psalm 56:3).

Although promises of God's protection are echoed many times throughout the pages of the Bible, there is no single passage that captures God's wonderful ability and desire to deliver His people in times of danger better than Psalm 91.

Every verse in this psalm is worth studying, but in this Evening Connection, we'll focus on the first seven verses.

> He who dwells in the secret place of the Most High shall abide under the shadow of the Almighty. I will say of The LORD, "He is my refuge and my fortress; My God, in Him I will trust." Surely He shall deliver you from the snare of the fowler and from the perilous pestilence. He shall cover you with His feathers, and under His wings you shall take refuge; His truth shall be your shield and buckler. You shall not be afraid of the terror by night, nor of the arrow that flies by day, nor of the pestilence that walks in darkness, nor of the destruction that lays waste at noonday. A thousand may fall at your side, and ten thousand at your right hand; but it shall not come near you *(New King James Version)*.

Those verses prove that God declares the end from the beginning! Thousands of years ago, He saw our day coming. He knew the exact dangers and challenges that would confront us today, and He specifically promised to protect us from them.

In fact, God promised to be our refuge. A *refuge* can be defined as "that which provides shelter or protection from danger, distress or calamity; a stronghold which protects by its strength; a sanctuary which secures safety by its sacredness; any place inaccessible to the enemy."

Doesn't it comfort you to know you can live in a place that's so secure, it's inaccessible to your enemy?

Certainly, that would include any human enemy. But what's more important, it includes our real enemy—Satan. He is the one behind every evil plot. He is the one who's come to steal, kill and destroy (John 10:10)—to terrorize you as Kenneth said, on the first day of this LifeLine Kit. But Psalm 91 tells us, when we trust God as our refuge, the devil can't touch us.

One commentary says that the person who takes refuge in the secret place of the Most High "will be enveloped by God's providence so that he can continue to seek holiness and wisdom without fear of those who would seek to do him harm."[11]

I particularly like that phrase "enveloped by God's providence" because it expresses the kind of comprehensive protection depicted again and again in Psalm 91. Verse 4, for example, says God will cover us with His feathers, and under His wings will we trust and find refuge. If you've ever seen a mother hen gather her chicks under her wings, you know that she draws them so close to her and covers them so completely that they all but disappear beneath her outstretched wings.

That's how thoroughly God takes care of us! He so covers us with His mighty, protective arms that no harm can even come near us, our families or our loved ones.

God promised that kind of protection to His people under the Old Covenant, and He promises it to us as His people under the New Covenant today. Starting this evening, begin thanking God for His divine protection in your life and the lives of your family members. You don't have to worry about tomorrow because as you abide in The WORD of God and obey Him, you can trust Him to protect you spirit, soul and body!

11 *Tehillim, A New Translation With a Commentary Anthologized From Talmudic, Midrashic and Rabbinic Sources,* the Artscoll Tanach Series, Two Volume Edition (New York: Mesorah Publications, Ltd., 2002) p. 1134.

Notes:

_____

_____

_____

_____

_____

_____

_____

_____

_____

_____

_____

_____

Evening  Reflection

In your own words, define *refuge*.

_____

_____

_____

How does God promise to be a refuge for you and your family?

_____

_____

_____

How does this revelation that God is your refuge affect how you think about the situations that cause you stress? How will it affect your day-to-day life? Be specific.

_____

_____

_____

Today's  Prayer of Faith

Father, I thank You that my family and I can dwell in Your secret place of protection. I thank You that Your WORD can defeat the tools of fear and worry and lead me into a place of safety and peace—spirit, soul and body. LORD, I will continue to trust in You and abide in Your WORD so that I may know You and live a life that honors You. In Jesus' Name, Amen!

Real-Life Testimonies
to Help Build Your Faith

God's Promise of Protection

Toward the end of 2007, I was up praying in the early morning and noticed the dark sky turning slightly pink. This is not the color we like to see here in Malibu, Calif. The winds had come up the day before, warm and strong. By 5:30 a.m. the dark sky had turned very pink. I began to take authority over fires and the wind, speaking God's protection and His words that state He has given us a strong, fenced, fortified city. I heard sirens around 6 a.m., and the hill directly above our condo complex was on fire.

Within minutes, the firemen were at our door telling us we had to evacuate immediately. Moments before the evacuation order came, a tremendous peace came over me. Four days later, we returned to our home. We had spent those four days mostly praying in the spirit. The fires burned ferociously and moved so rapidly, but we had no loss of lives and only eight structures destroyed in the 4500 acres that burned. The fire was 100 percent contained within five days. The fire burned all around our home and right up to the walls and patios of our condo complex but there was no damage to any of our buildings.

J.L.H.
California

Notes:

Chapter Four

Everything You Know About Suffering Isn't True

What Suffering Bought You
by Kenneth Copeland

Today, we're going to dive deeper into the price Jesus paid on the cross. That may seem far away from your life today, with bills to pay and other financial, family and job pressures, but I assure you, it is very relevant.

We've already discussed how Satan uses fear, stress, anxiety and/or depression to try to control you. Then, Gloria shared how you can enjoy the peace that comes from abiding, or remaining, in The LORD's divine protection. In this Morning Connection, I want to go into deeper study about the destruction of Satan's authority. Hebrews tells us:

> Forasmuch then as the children are partakers of flesh and blood, he [Jesus] also himself likewise took part of the same; that through death he might destroy him that had the power of death, that is, the devil; and deliver them who through fear of death were all their lifetime subject to bondage (Hebrews 2:14-15).

What we have just read is the most important news any believer could possibly receive. This report from God's WORD says the master terrorist (the devil) has been *destroyed* and the believer has been delivered from fear and every symptom associated with it, like stress, anxiety and/or depression.

The world is preoccupied with fear because apart from the cross of Jesus and His victory over death, no one can get rid of it. However, the person who has received total deliverance from the fear, stress, anxiety and/or depression that salvation provides, never again has to live in their grip or allow them any place in his or her thinking.

But how did this great deliverance take place? And how do we personally live totally delivered from fear and its symptoms?

To answer these questions we must, first of all, notice that we are talking about a flesh-and-blood victory here. Jesus poured His blood out for us. He allowed His flesh to be stripped and whipped for us. For what?

To defeat him who *had* the power of death. Pay attention to that verb "had." It is past tense. The devil no longer has the power of death over those who believe.

But notice, Jesus didn't just stop with victory over the devil. Jesus both *destroyed* him who had the power of death, "*and* deliver[ed] them who through fear of death were all their lifetime subject to bondage." That's you and me!

Look closely at what it says Jesus' suffering and victory purchased for us. It does not say that He gave us the power and ability to *cope* with fear, stress, anxiety and/or depression. Nor does it say that He gave us the power and the ability to choose which fear was good and which fear was bad.

No! It says He *delivered* us from fear.

And, He did it at the same time He purchased our salvation. Every believer is familiar with some of the victories that Jesus won at Calvary. We know that on the Cross, He bore our sins and delivered us from continued subjection to sin. And, we know that in His suffering and death, Jesus "took our infirmities, and bare our sicknesses" (Matthew 8:17; Isaiah 53:4-9).

What believers haven't yet fully applied in their lives is the truth that Jesus also took the power of death away from the devil. He did it by destroying Satan and pulling him down from his position of authority at the same time, and in the same act that delivered you and me from sin and sickness.

To get a better understanding of how Jesus' victory affects us, let's look at Romans 8:14-18:

> And if children, then heirs; heirs of God, and joint-heirs with Christ; if so be that we suffer with him, that we may be also glorified together. For I reckon that the sufferings of this present time are not worthy to be compared with the glory which shall be revealed in us.

These verses have been sadly misunderstood. We have been taught that the things we are suffering may be part of God's will for our lives, instead of recognizing them for what they are—the acts and deceptions of a desperate and defeated enemy.

In fact, the suffering referred to in those verses is not physical suffering at all. We can see that in just the first few words: "If so be that we suffer with him…." We don't suffer with Jesus on the cross. He suffered on the Cross in order to deliver us from the things He suffered.

To find out how believers do suffer with Jesus, look back again to Hebrews 2. There we will see that Jesus endured two different types of suffering. The first of these is described in verses 9-10:

> But we see Jesus, who was made a little lower than the angels for the suffering of death, crowned with glory and honour; that he by the grace of God should taste death for every man. For it became him, for whom are all things, and by whom are all things, in bringing many sons unto glory, to make the captain of their salvation perfect *through sufferings*.

Clearly, Jesus being made "perfect through sufferings" refers to Jesus suffering death so we could live. This suffering He endured in His body is not something we can share with Him, but a suffering He endured so we would not have to endure it.

If we do not share that type of suffering in the body with Jesus, then there must be another type of suffering we do suffer with Him. The WORD reveals what that suffering is:

For verily he took not on him the nature of angels; but he took on him the seed of Abraham. Wherefore in all things it behooved him to be made like unto his brethren, that he might be a merciful and faithful high priest in things pertaining to God, to make reconciliation for the sins of the people. For in that he himself hath *suffered being tempted,* he is able to succour them that are tempted (Hebrews 2:16-18).

The last verse is our key to the only kind of suffering that God intends His children to suffer with Jesus—temptation. And because He did, He is able to "succour" or "help" them that are tempted.

Jesus resisted the pressure and the temptation to sin and break fellowship with God. Jesus resisted by standing in faith on God's WORD and choosing to speak and do only what He heard and saw His Father say and do.

Hebrews 4:15 says Jesus was tempted in every way that we are—yet He did not sin. He faced Satan exactly like we face him. His suffering was that He resisted the same temptations we face, and more, in His life on earth.

The suffering we face does not require us to give in to fear, stress, anxiety and/or depression. Instead, our suffering takes place when we resist those counterfeits we discussed in Chapter 2. We suffer when we take a stand in faith regardless of what our relatives and friends say. We suffer when we choose to believe The WORD instead of what the world thinks.

Jesus suffered so that you don't have to endure stress, anxiety and/or depression. That's good news! When you understand that, you go from suffering to joy, from pressure to deliverance. And, it all begins when you quit treating fear, stress, anxiety and/or depression as a member of the family and start walking free from all bondage: free—as one who has been adopted by blood into the family of God.

Morning
Reflection

What is suffering according to God's WORD?

_____

_____

_____

What is the only kind of suffering you should stand against and over-come as a believer?

_____

_____

_____

How does this definition differ from what you previously understood _suffering_ **to be?**

_____

_____

_____

Today's
Connection Points

⊙ **_Selections From Peaceful Praise_ CD: "You Are My Hiding Place" (Track 4)**

Hide yourself in Him wherever you are today, by filling your heart with praise and songs of deliverance!

⊙ **DVD: "We Are Overcomers" (Chapter 4)**

Because you're born of God into covenant with Him, you're already a world overcomer. His faith, resident in you, is the victory that overcomes every challenge!

⊙ **Scriptures CD (Track 4)**

Isaiah 53:4-9; Romans 8:17-18; Hebrews 2:9-10, 16-18; 1 John 5:4, _The Amplified Bible;_ Colossians 1:12-13, _The Amplified Bible_

Faith  in Action

Resist the temptation to accept fear, stress, anxiety and/or depression as godly suffering. Instead, understand that Jesus has paid the price for your freedom from these counterfeits.

Put It Into Practice

Get Moving![12]

Throughout this LifeLine Kit, you are learning how to eradicate stress, anxiety and/or depression from your life with The WORD of God. There are practical steps you can take to assist with your healing. Exercise is one of those steps. If you have avoided exercise in the past, today is a new day. Just look at these benefits:

1. During exercise, your brain releases endorphins, chemicals that leave you feeling happier and more energized.
2. Physical activity helps to loosen muscle tension.
3. Exercise boosts your immune system while decreasing chemicals that cause feelings of depression and sadness.
4. Getting active reduces fatigue and increases alertness.
5. When you combine exercise with the outdoors, you get a combo deal—physical fitness, fresh air and a dose of vitamin D, a nutrient that may decrease depression while boosting your immune system.

Begin to make physical exercise part of your daily routine. Remember, it doesn't have to be strenuous, just 30 minutes each day—a walk around the block after dinner, gardening, playing with your dog or going on a bike ride with your children.[13] Don't wait another day to get up and get moving!

12 "Diseases and Conditions: Depression (major depressive disorder)" Mayo Clinic Staff, *Mayo Clinic*, http://www.mayoclinic.org/diseases-conditions/depression/in-depth/depression-and-exercise/art-20046495, (5/12/2015); "Exercise for Stress and Anxiety," *Anxiety and Depression Association of America*, http://www.adaa.org/living-with-anxiety/managing-anxiety/exercise-stress-and-anxiety (2/15/2015); "Depression," *Vitamin D Council*, https://www.vitamindcouncil.org/health-conditions/depression (5/12/2015).

13 "Your Exercise Routine: How Much Is Enough," Heather Hatfield, *Web MD*, http://www.webmd.com/fitness-exercise/guide/your-exercise-routine-how-much-is-enough (5/12/2015).

The Lie of Suffering
by Gloria Copeland

I want to continue the teaching on suffering that Kenneth began in today's Morning Connection. You see, years ago, the devil started a rumor. He told a few Christians that as long as they lived in the world, they had to suffer as the world did. He told them they had to share the diseases and defeat, the poverty and failure of those around them. He told them to not even hope to escape those things (not until they got to heaven, anyway) and, that to do so would be selfish.

It was a crafty lie, and it worked. Believers accepted it and began to spread it among themselves. You may have even heard it yourself. If so, I want to help you put that rumor to rest. I want to help you get the facts straight, once and for all.

You see, despite what you may have heard, health, prosperity and victorious living aren't concepts that some comfort-hungry believer selfishly dreamed up. They're *God's* ideas.

Since the beginning of time, God has desired for His family on earth to enjoy those things. He's longed for a people who would take Him up on His many gracious promises and live in victory over the beggarly elements of this world. And, through The LORD Jesus Christ, He's made it possible for us to do that. As 1 John 5:4 says, "Whatever is born of God is victorious over the world; and this is the victory that conquers the world, even our faith" *(The Amplified Bible)*.

The simple truth is, if you're born of God, you've got what it takes to live in victory. Don't let the devil talk you into anything less!

You may say, "That sounds good, Gloria, but we've got to be realistic. We live in a world full of problems. And as long as we live in this world, it seems to me we're going to have our share of them."

Yes, that's true. Even Jesus said, "In the world you have tribulation and trials and distress and frustration…." But notice, He didn't stop there! He went on to say, "…but be of good cheer [take courage; be confident, certain, undaunted]! For I have overcome the world. [I have deprived it of power to harm you and have conquered it for you]" (John 16:33, *The Amplified Bible*).

Most believers don't have any trouble believing the first part of that verse. They know all too well how many tribulations, trials, distresses and frustrations surround them. But they're less certain about the last part. They haven't yet experienced for themselves exactly what Jesus meant when He said He had deprived those things of the power to harm them. And, the reason they haven't had that experience is because they're still living as though they're part of the world.

You see, there are two kingdoms in operation on this earth: There's the kingdom of darkness and the kingdom of light. As children of God, you and I are citizens of the kingdom of light—even though we're surrounded by darkness.

Some people make the mistake of thinking they won't be able to live in the kingdom of light until they die and go to heaven. But that's not the case. Colossians 1:12-13 makes that clear. It says: "Giving thanks unto the Father, which hath made us meet to be partakers of the inheritance of the saints in light: who hath delivered us from the power of darkness, and hath translated us into the kingdom of his dear Son...."

Notice that the verbs in those verses are *past tense*. That's because your transference into the kingdom of light isn't something that's going to happen to you someday in the future. It's something that happened to you the day you made Jesus The LORD of your life. You've already been brought out of the darkness into the light.

Yes, even though your feet are firmly planted on the earth, as a born-again child of God, you are already a citizen of the kingdom of heaven. And, that citizenship gives you certain rights—including the right to experience victory over all the evils of this world.

You are, however, as Jesus said, to be "sanctified" or separated from them.

It's The WORD of God that separates you from the world. It's His WORD and His WORD alone that will set your victory into motion. If you'll receive it, believe it, speak it and act on it, that WORD will set you apart from those around you. It will take you from trouble to triumph, from anxiety to peace of mind, again and again.

We already found in 1 John 5:4 that "...this is the victory that overcometh the world, even our faith." Well since faith comes by hearing and hearing by The WORD of God, we could also say that scripture this way: "This is the victory that overcometh the world, even our believing God's WORD."

Faith is believing God's WORD under any circumstances (and usually *in spite of* the circumstances). It's believing God's promises of prosperity in spite of the negative balance in your bank account. It's believing God's promises of healing in spite of the pain.

I know that sounds tough, and it is at first. But anyone who's lived by faith for very long will tell you that if you'll just keep on feeding your mind and your heart with The WORD of God, one day that WORD will start to take hold inside you. You may be facing some obstacle that you haven't quite been able to conquer. You may have prayed about it and read The WORD and yet still struggled with doubts.

But if you will just keep at it, one day the reality of God's WORD concerning that obstacle will start to dawn on you. And suddenly, that impossibility you've been dealing with will become a possibility. Victory, peace and stress-free living will start to well up within you from the inside out.

Evening
Reflection

In your own words, define victorious living and peace of mind.

_____

_____

_____

Why are you entitled to live without stress, anxiety and/or depression?

_____

_____

_____

How does faith affect your ability to live victoriously?

_____

_____

_____

Today's
Prayer of Faith

Father, I thank You that according to Your WORD and the blood of Jesus, I am free—free from stress, anxiety and/ or depression. I thank You that my family, my health, my future, my money and my ministry belong to You. I pray that You will continue to help me walk in that truth and in Your BLESSING, every day! In Jesus' Name. Amen.

Real-Life Testimonies
to Help Build Your Faith

Believed and Received

Thank God for His Son, Jesus, who gave us authority to cast out devils and heal the sick. Last December I discovered a lump in my breast. It was as hard as a rock. I did not have fear at all. I was in peace knowing who I am in Christ. I praised God and thanked Him for the authority He gave me to speak to the mountain.

I spoke harshly to the lump and commanded it to die in the Name of Jesus. I cursed the roots of that lump just like Jesus cursed that fig tree. From there, I praised The LORD every time I would think about it. Guess what? It disappeared in less than a week. I am free! My husband could not believe it since he wanted it to be taken care of through doctors. It's according to your faith and revelation! Hallelujah!

M.S.
London

Notes:

Chapter Five
De-Stressing Stress

Choose God's Way
by Kenneth Copeland

This morning I want to talk to you about choosing God's way versus the world's way. First, let's talk about the world's way. This system flows in a negative, downhill, destructive stream. Just turn on your local news, and you'll see what I mean. Satan has trained many of us to operate in the negative. We talk fear all the time and, for the most part, are totally unaware of it. The danger is that by giving thought, words and action to it, the force of fear works proficiently and continues to work as long as we allow it. Anyone who is overcoming stress, anxiety and/or depression needs to be aware of these dangers and realize that by giving our thoughts, words and actions to fear, we empower it against us. Thankfully, stopping is possible.

Of course, some people think a little fear is healthy, but that's a lie! There is no such thing as healthy fear! Fear is part of the world's, or Satan's way, and there is no such thing as a combination of God's way and Satan's way. There is only one method of operation and one set of laws that fulfill and bring peace: God's way and God's WORD!

To better understand the two systems, let's look at the two opposing forces that exist in the earth—faith and fear. Understanding faith allows us to better understand fear. But what exactly is faith? It is the substance of things hoped for and the evidence of things not yet seen with the physical eye (Hebrews 11:1). It is the force that reaches out into the unreality of things you need, into the world of the spirit (heaven's supply), and brings those things into physical manifestation.

How does The WORD of God tell us that faith works? "Faith cometh by hearing, and hearing by The WORD of God" (Romans 10:17). And, Galatians 5:6 says faith works by love.

Faith is developed by meditating on God's WORD and by acting on that WORD. Meditating on The WORD causes the capacity for faith to increase. By meditating on it and practicing it, The WORD produces the results of faith, love, healing, prosperity, wisdom, well-being and peace in every area—spirit, soul and body.

I remember an incident that occurred with a friend of mine. He called my mother in the middle of the night in desperate need of prayer. He was in the hospital for surgery, but fear had taken control of him to such an extent that the doctors wouldn't administer the anesthetic. One of them said, "This man has too much fear in him." They would not administer the anesthetic nor would they do surgery on him, or anyone else, when that much fear was present. They said he probably would have died.

My mother went to the hospital and laid hands on him. She spoke to that fear in the Name of Jesus, and drove it out. They still haven't operated on him to this day. He is well. Praise God!

I share this story with you because the more you meditate on fear, the more it will grow in your life. You will begin to speak of things that haven't happened as though they already have. Stress, anxiety and panic will grow, and eventually depression will take up residence. Then, you will act on that fear and it will bring the results of the curse of the law, which is bondage. But you don't have to act on fear. You don't have to practice fear. You don't have to talk fear. Give it *no* place! If you sense it rising up within you, stop right then, take authority over it in Jesus' Name, and cast it out.

When you speak to a mountain in faith as in Mark 11:23-24, you put the invisible force of God's creative power to work. When faith-filled words come out of your mouth, they are backed by the Spirit of God and the angels of God. All that power is applied to the mountain to remove it. You are the only one who can withdraw that power, and you do it by meditating on the lies of the devil and the words of the world. Then by setting into motion the force of fear, you add support to the mountain and build it up. As an act of your will, you allow fear to operate, and the result is defeat. A person of faith will meditate on God's WORD instead of worrying, and then he will speak to the mountain and say, "Be thou removed, and be thou cast into the sea." His next step is to support these faith words by acting on his faith and praising God until the mountain is completely gone.

You *can* step through the door from fear into absolute faith and put a stop to Satan's destructive maneuvers in your life. Stand up boldly and say, "I've been made the righteousness of Almighty God. I've been washed in the blood of the Lamb. The LORD is on my side; I *will* not fear. Sin shall have no dominion over me, stress shall have no dominion over me, anxiety and depression shall have no dominion over me. He that is within me is greater than he that is in the world. Jesus bore my sicknesses and carried my diseases. By His stripes, I am healed. Therefore, I boldly say that The LORD is my helper, and I will not fear. What can man do to me?"

Morning Reflection

How are faith and fear related?

_____

_____

_____

How do you build your faith?

_____

_____

_____

How do your words affect your faith? How do they affect your peace of mind?

_____

_____

_____

Today's Connection Points

⊙ _Selections From Peaceful Praise_ CD: "Be Still, My Soul" (Track 5)

Let the peace only God can give—the peace that transcends all understanding—quiet and mount guard over your heart and mind as you enter into worship and praise this morning.

⊙ DVD: "Living Totally Free From Fear" (Chapter 5)

His perfect love, flowing in you, through you and around you, casts out all fear, bondage and oppression. He loves you as much as He loves Jesus. Believe and yield to His unconditional love and acceptance today.

⊙Scriptures CD (Track 5)

Galatians 5:6; Psalm 118:6; Mark 11:23-26; 1 Corinthians 1:30; James 4:7, *The Amplified Bible*; John 14:21; Psalm 34:3-10; 2 Corinthians 10:4-5, *The Amplified Bible*; Isaiah 32:17-18

Faith in Action

Consider the situations that cause you stress, anxiety and/or depression.
How do you respond to them? How can you change the way you respond to them?

Put It Into Practice

Plan for Peace

Planning is an important part of putting your mind at ease. Whether you are planning to make your day more successful or planning for a loved one's long-term care, getting a plan in place and then acting on it is the best way to achieve your goals. In fact, Proverbs 21:5 *(New Living Translation)* says that "good planning and hard work lead to prosperity." To make your plans succeed, put these steps into practice:

1. Prayerfully consider your end goal.
   What do you really want or need? Do you need to feel more successful in your day? Do you need more rest or more joy? Do you need a solution to a parent's living situation? Be clear on your goal, and write it down. As The WORD encourages in Habakkuk 2:2: "Write the vision, and make it plain upon tables, that he may run that readeth it."

2. List the steps you need to take to achieve your goal.
   Again, this takes prayer. Begin listing out all the things you know need to happen for the end goal to occur. Do you need to research care facilities? Do you need outside help with your household or business? No matter how small the step may be, list it.

3. Get wise counsel.
   If you don't know the steps you need to take, then turn to trusted leaders, spiri-

tually mature friends and even industry associations for suggestions. Proverbs 15:22 says, "Without counsel purposes are disappointed: but in the multitude of counsellors they are established." Whether you need help coming up with strategies for relaxing during your busy day or help caring for an aging parent, you can find support and guidance from others who have experience in that area.

4.   Create a day-to-day or week-to-week plan.
     Now that you have your to-do list, begin listing it out in order. Choose three things that need to be completed by a certain day—either per day or per week. If you are looking to feel more successful from day to day, then choose the three things that would make you feel most successful each day if you were to accomplish those, and do them first. If you are planning for a parent's new living situation, then plan the three things that need to be completed this week and do those. Taking small steps will add up quickly to success.

5.   Be realistic and patient.
     It may take time for you to experience the benefits of proper planning, but don't give up. Be realistic about what you can accomplish from day to day, week to week, and be patient to know that God will bless your efforts. As The WORD says in Proverbs 16:3: "Commit thy works unto The LORD, and thy thoughts shall be established." Through godly planning and patience, the results will come.

Begin putting these steps into practice, today. Don't let difficult situations and chaos rule your life. Take a godly approach to planning, and enjoy a more peaceful and productive life!

Notes:

_____

_____

_____

_____

_____

_____

_____

_____

_____

_____

_____

Freedom Through Forgiveness
by Kenneth Copeland

There's nothing in the world more practical and predictable than faith in God's WORD. It always produces dependable, consistent results. When we use it the way God designed it, living by faith is much like driving a car. All we have to do is follow the manufacturer's instructions and our faith gets us wherever we want to go—all the time, every time—without fail.

If it doesn't, it's because something is out of line. It's not because God in His sovereignty just decided to put His foot on the brake. It's not because, as some people say, "He works in mysterious ways, and you just never know what He's going to do." It's because there's a problem somewhere.

Most of us understand this when it comes to our automobiles. If we put the key in the ignition, turn it and nothing happens, we don't just shake our heads and say, "Well, I guess it's just not the will of General Motors (or Toyota, Chevrolet or whatever) that I go anywhere today. I guess I'm just meant to stay home."

No, we say, "Hey, what's wrong here?" Then we check the gas gauge, look under the hood or call a mechanic because we know we're not going anywhere until we identify the problem and get it fixed.

We ought to respond much the same way when our faith fails to function properly. If we pray and believe God for something and don't get results, we should grab our faith manual—the Bible—and find out what's messing up the system. One of the first verses we should look at is John 14:21 where Jesus said, "He that hath my commandments, and keepeth them, he it is that loveth me: and he that loveth me shall be loved of my Father, and I will love him, and will manifest myself to him."

Right there, in that one scripture, we can see how to fix almost any seeming "faith failure." We do it by *having* and *keeping* Jesus' commandments; by *hearing, believing* and *obeying* His WORD. When we do those things, He can manifest Himself to us. And, when Jesus is in manifestation, our faith always gets results!

Don't confuse this with legalism that requires us to earn things from God. Jesus already earned everything for us and made us His joint heirs. Through Him, every spiritual blessing in heavenly places and every promise God made is ours just because we're born again. That's the beauty of the New Covenant. It has empowered us and set us free, not to disregard Jesus' commandments, but to keep them—*just because we love Him!*

Personally, I'm thrilled with the commands Jesus has given me—especially the ones about faith. That's why one of my favorite passages in the Bible is Mark 11:22-26 where Jesus said:

> Have faith in God. For verily I say unto you, That whosoever shall say unto this mountain, Be thou removed, and be thou cast into the sea; and shall not doubt in his heart, but shall believe that those things which he saith shall come to pass; he shall have whatsoever he saith. Therefore I say unto you, What things soever ye desire, when ye pray, believe that ye receive them, and ye shall have them. And when ye stand praying, forgive, if ye have ought against any: that your Father also which is in heaven may forgive you your trespasses. But if ye do not forgive, neither will your Father which is in heaven forgive your trespasses.

Jesus gave us a number of commands in those verses. First, He told us to "have faith in God," or, "have the God kind of faith."[14] What is the God kind of faith? It's the same kind Jesus has. It's the kind of faith He functioned in when He was on earth, which is the kind that always works.

Is it really possible for us to have that kind of faith? Yes, it is, and here's why: Jesus always authorizes and empowers us to do whatever He commands. Therefore, the very fact that He commanded us to have the God kind of faith—faith that speaks to mountains, and receives whatever it asks for in prayer—means He has authorized and empowered us to do it.

That's good news. It's worth shouting about!

But Jesus didn't stop there. He went on to say something else of major importance. He said, "When ye stand praying, forgive."

That is a huge command! Everything Jesus said about faith hangs on it because "faith...worketh by love" (Galatians 5:6), and forgiveness is an essential expression of love. Without forgiveness, faith won't function. It just sits there like a car with a dead battery, going nowhere.

Forgiveness is not a mental force. It's like faith: Feelings have nothing to do with it, one way or another. It's a spiritual force and is done as an act of obedience to Jesus, The LORD—HEAD OF THE CHURCH. It's not optional. It's a *command!*

Many Christians haven't understood this. They've had the idea that forgiveness is optional. "You just don't know what that person did to me!" they'll say. "I've been trying to forgive them for years but I haven't been able to do it. I guess I just need a little more time."

Such statements directly contradict what Jesus said. He didn't tell us to take years to forgive people. He commanded us to forgive them right now, immediately, while we're praying. He told us to do it before we say, "Amen!" Not because He's hardheaded, but because our faith (and therefore, the answer to our prayer) depends on it.

Listen to what Jesus said: "When you *stand* praying, forgive." You can't stand up for months or weeks. Make forgiveness part of every prayer.

"But, Brother Copeland, what if I don't have anything against anyone?"

14 See Mark 11:22 *Young's Literal Translation; The Bible in Basic English; Numeric English New Testament.*

Did you get angry, or put out, with politicians? Then, forgive. Stay with me, now. We're going to a much higher place with this.

Let's look at Matthew 9:2-7. You probably remember this story. A paralyzed man's friends couldn't get into the house where Jesus was preaching because there were too many people in it. So the friends ripped off part of the roof, put the man on a mat, and lowered him down into the meeting:

> And, behold, they brought to him a man sick of the palsy, lying on a bed: and Jesus seeing their faith said unto the sick of the palsy; Son, be of good cheer; thy sins be forgiven thee. And, behold, certain of the scribes said within themselves, This man blasphemeth. And Jesus knowing their thoughts said, Wherefore think ye evil in your hearts? For whether is easier, to say, Thy sins be forgiven thee; or to say, Arise, and walk? But that ye may know that the Son of man hath power on earth to forgive sins, (then saith he to the sick of the palsy,) Arise, take up thy bed, and go unto thine house. And he arose, and departed to his house.

That didn't go over very well, especially with the religious crowd. They thought, *This is blasphemy. Only God can forgive sins!* Mark's account of the same story says,

> And immediately when Jesus perceived in his spirit that they so reasoned within themselves, he said unto them, Why reason ye these things in your hearts? Whether is it easier to say to the sick of the palsy, Thy sins be forgiven thee; or to say, Arise, and take up thy bed, and walk? But that ye may know that the Son of man hath power on earth to forgive sins, (he saith to the sick of the palsy,) I say unto thee, Arise, and take up thy bed, and go thy way into thine house. And immediately he arose, took up the bed, and went forth before them all (chapter 2:8-12).

Do you see what happened there? Jesus declared and demonstrated the fact that *the power that forgives is exactly the same power that heals.*

On one hand, the power of forgiveness wipes out sin and, on the other, it heals and removes sickness and disease. Once that is made clear, it's very easy to see and understand the connection between them. Sickness and unforgiveness are both under the curse and tied together with death. No wonder The LORD is so strict about, "Forgive, and do it, NOW!"

Let's take another step up. Jesus, our example, said those powerful words: "Father, forgive them; for they know not what they do" (Luke 23:34). Those were not just wonderful words. They were, and are, POWER! They were a major part of the Resurrection!

In Matthew 27:25, listen to what the people said: "Then answered all the people, and said, His blood be on us, and on our children."

It was, and still is, Jesus' calling to forgive. That's His job! First John 4:17 makes it very clear that it's our job, too! "Herein is our love made perfect, that we may have boldness in the day of judgment: because as he is, so are we in this world."

Hebrews 3:1 says we are partakers of His calling. We have inherited, with Him, the authority and power to forgive. We are ministers of grace (Ephesians 4:29). Forgiveness is the first act of grace. Start forgiving everyone you see. Practice forgiving. While you're watching the news, forgive everyone—not just the bad guys—*everyone!*

Let's look at 2 Corinthians 5:17-19:

> Therefore if any man be in Christ, he is a new creature: old things are passed away; behold, all things are become new. And all things are of God, who hath reconciled us to himself by Jesus Christ, and hath given to us the ministry of reconciliation; to wit, that God was in Christ, reconciling the world unto himself, not imputing their trespasses unto them; and hath committed unto us the word of reconciliation.

Now, look at verse 19 in *The Amplified Bible:* "It was God [personally present] in Christ, reconciling and restoring the world to favor with Himself, not counting up and holding against [men] their trespasses [but cancelling them], and committing to us the message of reconciliation (of the restoration to favor)."

Jesus said, "Forgive them; for they know not what they do." If they knew, they would come running to Jesus. When the healing-forgiving force of grace is released through you and me, it begins to work in and on others. It will draw people to the source of that grace—THE LOVE of GOD!

To practice forgiveness is to practice healing. Pray this: "Father, in the Name of Jesus I yield to the command of Jesus to forgive. I give myself to You as an instrument of Your love and forgiveness. I yield to compassion—the same compassion that moved You when You were on the earth to forgive, heal the sick and raise the dead. I'm Yours to command."

Now, take it a step further and shout it: "I'm a forgiver! I'm not a condemner. I'm an instrument of God's grace. I'm a minister of grace!"

When you walk into a store, just say, "Thank You, LORD Jesus, for Your grace. I forgive everyone in this store. By faith, I release the power to heal on every person. If I may be of service to You and to someone here, I'm Yours!"

When you're driving say, "I forgive everyone on this highway." Teach this to your children and/or grandchildren. Teach them to say, every day: "I forgive every teacher and every student in this school."

Again, remember that *forgiveness is the same spiritual force as healing.* It's the same force as saving grace or eternal life—*ZOE* in Greek (the life of God). Jesus said, "I have come that you may have life and have it more abundantly" (John 10:10). We are forgiveness agents in the earth. We are THE BLESSED! That's what we are, and that's what we do!

The Bible calls that power *the anointing,* and it's a tangible, spiritual force. It's the force Jesus was talking about in Luke 4:18 when He said, "The Spirit of The LORD is upon me, because he hath anointed me to preach the gospel to the poor; he hath sent me to heal the brokenhearted, to preach deliverance to the captives, and recovering of sight to the blind, to set at liberty them that are bruised."

This burden-removing, yoke-destroying anointing is the power behind forgiveness. So when we refuse or neglect to forgive, we choke it off and hinder its operation in our lives.

That's dangerous business!

"I know, Brother Copeland," you might say, "but what if someone has hurt me so much, I can't even stand the thought of them? What am I supposed to do?"

Just obey Jesus. He didn't ask you to feel better about the person who wronged you. He commanded you to forgive them. Forgiveness isn't about feelings. It's an act of obedience. It's choosing to put God's WORD above your emotions by making a decision to say, "I forgive."

The quicker you do that, the better off you'll be.

The reverse is also true. The longer you wait, the worse things will get and the more deeply mired in unforgiveness you'll become.

You'll just be going along doing something else entirely, when suddenly you'll find yourself mentally rehearsing the ugly things someone did and said to you. You'll imagine yourself saying the things you wish you'd said at the time. With each rehearsal, the conversation in your head will get uglier. The negative effects will be re-energized. You'll relive the hurt and it will do more damage, trapping you in a cycle of stress, anxiety and/or depression.

Every one of us has done this at one time or another. We've all gotten caught in a cycle of unforgiveness and spent hours, days or even months, feeling angry and hurt and upset with someone. It's a miserable experience.

But, as born-again believers we don't have to get trapped in it anymore. Instead, we can do what Jesus commanded, and we can do it instantly. As soon as we realize we "have ought against any," while we stand praying, we can forgive!

We don't have to make a big production out of it, either. If there are other people around us at the time, we can just whisper quietly so no one else can hear, "LORD, I forgive that person." Thirty minutes later, if the negative thoughts come back to our minds again, we can say it again. "LORD, I'm not a condemner. I'm a forgiver—and I forgive."

Do you know what will happen when we do that?

The anointing will start flowing in that area of our lives. God's burden-removing, yoke-destroying power will go to work and give us insight into that troublesome situation. He'll show us what we can do to correct it. He'll start working in and through us to bring healing to everyone and everything involved.

And because we're walking in love, Jesus will be manifesting Himself to us, resulting in deliverance from stress, anxiety and/or depression. Our spiritual engine will be roaring, and our faith will be working just like God designed it—bringing His promises to pass for us and taking us wherever we want to go.

All the time! Every time! Without fail!

Evening
Reflection

Why is forgiveness so vital?

_____

_____

_____

How are forgiveness and healing alike? What do both require? See Mark 2:8-12.

_____

_____

_____

Who do you need to forgive? What scriptures will you stand on for that forgiveness to be complete in you, and what will you do when symptoms of unforgiveness try to creep back into your life?

_____

_____

_____

Notes:

_____

_____

_____

_____

_____

_____

_____

_____

_____

_____

_____

_____

Today's
Prayer of Faith

Father, I thank You for Your WORD. I trust that You are faithful to bring it to pass in my life—no matter what the situation. By faith, I choose to forgive those who have hurt me. I release the pain and anger, and I choose to walk in love toward them, just as You have loved me. By the blood of Jesus, I am a forgiver, not a condemner. In Jesus' Name. Amen.

Real-Life Testimonies
to Help Build Your Faith

No Respecter of Persons

Your ministry sent me Partner CDs of a testimony in 2009. One of the testimonies was about an Air Force mom whose son had parachuted out of a plane. His chute had failed to open, but he lived. The mom said she confessed that her son would live and testify to the glory of The LORD.

When I heard that I said out loud, "God is no respecter of persons, and what He did for her son, He will do for mine." This was right before my son was to deploy to Afghanistan. I stood on that verse and many others.

In 2009, my U.S. Marine son returned safely from Afghanistan after a 7 ½-month tour being on the front line. No one in his unit was seriously hurt. Praise God, this was all due to prayer and God's almighty protection. Thank you for your ministry that teaches how to stand on The WORD of God!

B.P.
Ohio

Chapter Six
How to Stop Worrying

Getting Rid of Worry
by Kenneth Copeland

There is no doubt in my mind that Jesus was speaking and prophesying of the very days in which we live when He said: "And ye shall hear of wars and rumours of wars: see that ye be not troubled: for all these things must come to pass, but the end is not yet. For nation shall rise against nation, and kingdom against kingdom: and there shall be famines, and pestilences, and earthquakes, in divers places" (Matthew 24:6-7).

He accurately describes all the challenging things we are surrounded by in our daily lives. However, as we work through today's Morning Connection, I want you to notice what He says right in the midst of describing all that trouble: "See that ye be not troubled." This is not a mild suggestion. It is a command: See to it that you're not troubled!

I am reminded of what Proverbs 4:23 says, "Keep thy heart with all diligence; for out of it are the issues (or forces) of life." Jesus is telling us to do something that seems impossible in bad times; but always remember that you, the believer, can do whatever The WORD says. You *can't* do it in your own strength, but you can do it in the strength of God with Jesus as your helper.

Jesus says we are to see to it that we are not troubled or worried. Let's discuss some of the things we can do to keep from being troubled. First of all, you must take the time to get your thinking in line with The WORD of God. That is an absolute must! You must continually feed on The WORD instead of on the elements of this world. I have learned the importance of reminding myself that Jesus, The LORD-Head of the Church, is still in absolute charge and control. It's easy to think that the devil has control, but he doesn't. Satan makes a lot of headlines, but God always wins the wars!

You need to learn to keep your priorities in proper order. A good way to do this is to check your heart and see if you are troubled on the inside. Are you troubled over our school system? Is there fear deep in you because of the obvious failures of our educational system? If the answer is yes, then your priorities are in the wrong place. Education has never been our salvation. You need to spend time in prayer for our teachers instead of worrying about them.

Is there fear and trouble in you because of our political failures? If so, then your priorities are not right. Political power is not the key to our salvation—Jesus is! Begin to take the time to pray for our leaders instead of criticizing them. According to 1 Timothy 2:1-2 we are to pray first of all for those in authority over us. When we do, then the result will be a life of quietness and peace.

In Mark 4:24, Jesus said to His disciples: "Take heed what ye hear: with what measure ye mete, it shall be measured to you: and unto you that hear shall more be given."

What are you hearing? There is all sorts of information being published abroad. So what are you hearing? Are you hearing talk of financial disaster? Are you hearing reports of sickness and disease? Are you hearing of wars and rumors of wars? The plain fact is that you are hearing whatever you have decided to hear. And, what you decide to hear is exactly what you will have.

Just about everywhere you look these days, you see signs of shortage, disaster and general despair. Thank God, this is not the attitude of the believer who is actively living by faith. We need to be watchful how we react to surrounding circumstances. The key is to respond with God's WORD, not with fear, worry or anxiety. Through His WORD, we draw strength from Him.

Understand, we don't have to worry because we are not of this world, and our God meets our needs "according to His riches in glory by Christ Jesus" (Philippians 4:19). We can always be confident in our God and His WORD, and allow the Holy Spirit to use our testimony to share His truth with the world.

Morning Reflection

Write Proverbs 4:23 on the lines below. What comes out of your heart?

_____

_____

_____

What are two things you can do to see to it that you are not troubled or worried?

_____

_____

_____

What is the key to responding to the circumstances surrounding us?

_____

_____

_____

Today's
Connection Points

- ### *Selections From Peaceful Praise* **CD: "My Peace" (Track 6)**

  Jesus has given you His peace. The world's "peace" is short-lived and incomplete, but as you listen to this morning's selection, allow the complete peace only He can give to flood your spirit, soul and body.

- ### DVD: "The Faith Connection" (Chapter 6)

  God's WORD is filled with His faith—the anointing connection that removes burdens and destroys yokes. Connect with the power in His WORD today, and walk free from every fear and bondage!

- ### Scriptures CD (Track 6)

  1 Peter 5:7, *The Amplified Bible;* Matthew 24:6-7; 1 Timothy 2:1-2; Mark 4:24; Philippians 4:19; Psalms 4:8, 127:2; 145:9; Matthew 6:25-27, *The Amplified Bible;* Proverbs 16:3, *The Amplified Bible;* Matthew 6:33; Joshua 1:8

Faith
in Action

Pay close attention to the words you speak today. Do they build up or tear down? Do they create worry, or are they an expression of your faith in God?

Begin replacing opportunities to worry with praise and The WORD.

Put It Into
Practice

Restore and Rejuvenate

Let's talk sleep. Are you getting enough? Is the sleep you're getting good, restful and replenishing? God created sleep as an integral part of the spirit, soul and body connection He put in place (Psalms 4:8, 127:2). Just look at the benefits[15] He designed for sleep to give you:

- Sleep stimulates your brain to improve your mood and combat stress and anxiety
- Sleep restores your body by reducing inflammation
- Sleep boosts your immune system
- Sleep improves your memory as well as your ability to learn, study and be creative
- Sleep makes it more likely for you to maintain a healthy weight by regulating the hormones that cause hunger and satiety, or fullness
- Sleeps helps regulate blood sugar.

What constitutes healthy sleep? Healthy sleep generally includes seven to eight hours of uninterrupted sleep per night. However, this number may differ for you. So take note of how you feel with different amounts of sleep. Do you feel rested after six hours of sleep, whereas seven leaves you groggy? Or maybe you feel stronger with 8 ½ or nine hours of sleep. It's more important to follow how God designed your body than to follow a list. And, if you need help achieving better sleep, try these tips:

1. **Stick to a schedule.**
   Go to bed and wake up at the same time each day instead of allowing your bedtimes/wake times to fluctuate.

2. **Create a bedtime routine.**
   Over time, by following a bedtime routine, your body will begin to prepare for sleep the closer you get to lights out. This could include taking a warm bath or shower, reading before lights out or deep-breathing exercises.

3. **Watch your diet.**
   Avoid caffeine, a key ingredient in coffee, tea and chocolate, which can either make it hard to fall asleep or wake you up during the night. Also avoid foods and drinks that will cause you to feel sluggish when you wake up.

4. **Protect your sleep space.**
   Avoid taking work and media into your bedroom. Both of these can stimulate your brain and make falling asleep more difficult.

Commit to improving your sleep as you work through this LifeLine Kit. Realize that God created you as a whole person—spirit, soul and body. Those three areas affect each other. So as you are strengthening your spirit, strengthen your mind and body with better sleep. This will, in turn, strengthen your spirit and help you achieve a more peaceful life.

15 "Why Is Sleep Important?," National Institute of Health: National Heart, Lung and Blood Institute, http://www.nhlbi.nih.gov/health/health-topics/topics/sdd/why.html, (2/15/2015).

Worry Won't Get You What You Need…but God Will!

by Gloria Copeland

Sitting in the kitchen in the cold of winter, I have seen a bird and thought, *God has put Himself on the line to provide for that bird!*

Then, I found myself going out and throwing it something to eat.

Do you know that in all the times I've done that, I have never seen a bird look worried about where his next meal would come from? God said He would provide for the birds, and He keeps His WORD.

So let me ask you: Are you worried? Do you feel like you're spinning your wheels trying to get the things you need? If so, then you aren't living in a revelation of the goodness of God and His willingness to bless you. You aren't following Jesus' instructions in Matthew 6 to receive the good things God has laid up for you.

Time after time, the Bible talks about God's goodness. Psalm 145:9 sums it up this way: "The LORD is good to all."

You may think, *But I've already heard that God is good and He wants to bless me.*

Then why are you worrying instead of receiving?

Many people believe God is good, but head knowledge alone doesn't affect their daily lives. It takes more than head knowledge to change your circumstances—it takes a revelation from The WORD of God.

Do you know what a revelation is? It's a truth that becomes so real to you, as the Holy Spirit shines light on it, that it becomes a part of your life. You don't just hear it and then forget about it. You act on it. It is knowledge acted on that brings results.

This is what happened to me years ago when this passage in Matthew 6 became my first encounter with a revelation from The WORD of God. I had come by worry naturally. I had been raised in a church where they didn't really think God was interested or would get involved in their lives. As a result, they worried about everything—and they taught me to worry. It became such a habit that it seemed irresponsible *not* to worry.

But when I read that God was even interested in the birds, I knew He must care about me! This scripture helped build my faith. It became a revelation to me, and I asked God to take my life and do something with it. I found out that when you give God just a little opening, He will come right in.

When I had this experience, *The Amplified Bible* had just been published. Two friends and I would meet every week and read it together, not knowing any better than to just believe what it said. It was from these verses that I received the revelation that we are not to worry:

> Therefore I tell you, stop being perpetually uneasy (anxious and worried) about your life, what you shall eat or what you shall drink; or about your body, what you shall put on. Is not life greater [in quality] than food, and the body [far above and more excellent] than clothing? Look at the birds of the air; they neither sow nor reap nor gather into barns, and yet your heavenly Father keeps feeding them. Are you not worth much more than they? And who of you by worrying and being anxious can add one unit of measure (cubit) to his stature or to the span of his life? (Matthew 6:25-27, *The Amplified Bible*).

Another scripture that really helped me was Proverbs 16:3: "Roll your works upon The LORD [commit and trust them wholly to Him; He will cause your thoughts to become agreeable to His will, and] so shall your plans be established and succeed" *(The Amplified Bible)*.

Now understand, just because I received revelation about worry doesn't mean the temptation to worry immediately left me. When I took hold of these scriptures, I had to *learn* not to worry.

Minute by minute I would reject worried thoughts that came at me from every direction. Though I didn't know it at the time, I was doing what 2 Corinthians 10:5 says. I was "casting down imaginations, and every high thing that exalteth itself against the knowledge of God, and bringing into captivity every thought to the obedience of Christ."

At the time, Ken and I were in desperate need of all kinds of things. We were drowning in a sea of debt and trouble, and The WORD became our life preserver! I had read in Matthew 6:33 that if I would seek God first, He would take care of the "things." This was such good news to me. I wanted to learn more.

My way out of worry and into the reality of God's goodness all started with one scripture. Proverbs 7:2 says to keep The WORD as "the apple of thine eye." That means it should always be the center of your focus. The WORD is what you center your life around if you want to live the good life God has for you. It has to be No. 1.

I would like to say this is always easy. But, it's not.

In this busy world, what is easy is to get our priorities out of order. We can become so caught up in the cares of daily life that we don't make time for God and His kingdom.

So how do you stop worrying? *You replace worrying with believing what The WORD says.* You refuse to worry.

Run to The WORD of God and feed on it day and night. Find scriptures that apply to your situation. Keep them in front of your eyes, and going in your ears and your mouth, until that truth gets in your heart.

Joshua 1:8 says meditate on The WORD: "This book of the law shall not depart out of thy mouth; but thou shalt meditate therein day and night, that thou mayest observe to do according to all that is written therein: for then thou shalt make thy way prosperous, and then thou shalt have good success."

Meditation is more than just reading. It's fixing your mind on The WORD so that you *do* all that is written therein. You will gain revelation and insight into The WORD that you never could gain by only reading.

The next time you are tempted to worry, just look at a bird. Does it seem worried? No, it has a heavenly Father who cares about it.

Well, you have that same Father, and He delights in providing for you.

Remember, The LORD is good to *all*. So why worry?

Evening  Reflection

How do you combat worry?

_____

_____

_____

What does it mean to meditate on The WORD of God?

_____

_____

_____

What situations in your life are tempting you to worry? Find one to three scriptures on which to stand that specifically speak to each situation.

_____

_____

_____

Notes:

_____

_____

_____

_____

_____

_____

Today's
Prayer of Faith

Father, I trust You, and I trust in Your goodness. I believe just as You care for the birds, You care for me and the issues I face. I ask that whenever worry begins to creep into my thinking, Your Holy Spirit would bring it to my attention so I turn to Your WORD to think Your thoughts and speak Your words instead. In Jesus' Name. Amen!

Real-Life Testimonies
to Help Build Your Faith

Supernatural Debt Relief

I just want to give God glory for supernaturally bringing us out of a huge debt of close to six million pesos [around $150,000 U.S.]. As pastors, we had no way to pay off the debt with our small salary, but God did it! A company that owed my husband money 28 years ago, long before he became a pastor, finally paid us!

Our partnership with you is one of many reasons for the breakthrough. Glory to God! Thank you, Kenneth and Gloria Copeland. God bless you and your ministry!

Vicky M.
Philippines

Chapter Seven
Being Anxious for Nothing: The Force of Peace

Peace Is Possible
by Gloria Copeland

In this day and time, peace is a precious commodity. And, for many people, it's a rare one. Every day, our eyes, ears and hearts can be bombarded by the media with glaring headlines of doom and visions of turmoil...anything but peace. People everywhere are experiencing all kinds of pressure, stress, anxiety and/or depression. And, people every-where have a *choice* to make—to either receive turmoil into their hearts or to resist fear and refuse to allow it to chip away at their peace.

I feel confident *you* will choose to resist fear and live in peace—regardless of what's happening. And, there's only one way to effectively do that—you must go to God and His WORD.

A key scripture for being established in peace is found in Isaiah 26:3, "Thou wilt keep him in perfect peace, whose mind is stayed on thee: because he trusteth in thee." Peace comes as a result of trusting God—operating in faith, keeping your mind on His WORD and acting on it.

It's interesting to note that in this verse, the word for peace is *shalom,* which means "nothing missing, nothing broken." Its root word means "to be complete, sound, whole." And another definition for peace I especially like is: "everything that makes for man's highest good." Think about how that reveals God's heart—He has the "highest good" in mind for us.

That kind of peace means living in a state of rest, quietness and calmness. It is the absence of anxiety and strife—a place of tranquility. It generally denotes perfect well-being and includes harmonious relationships between God and man, and between people, nations and families.

Doesn't that motivate you to cultivate peace in your own life?

The 19th century minister, Alexander Maclaren, said: "True peace comes not from the absence of trouble, but from the presence of God and will be deep and passing all understanding in the exact measure in which we live in and partake of the love of God."[16]

Think about that for a minute...peace isn't determined by the absence of trouble but rather by the presence of God.

When trouble comes against us, we can rest in peace knowing that Jesus "was wounded for our transgressions, He was bruised for our guilt and iniquities; the chastisement [needful to obtain] peace and well-being for us was upon Him, and with the stripes [that wounded] Him we are healed and made whole" (Isaiah 53:5, *The Amplified Bible*).

Isn't it wonderful to know that Jesus bore all the bad things that could steal our peace—sin, grief, depression, anxiety, fear, mental illness and disease? He paid the price for us to live peacefully in this life!

But it's important to realize that peace doesn't come automatically—there is something for us to do. Yes, Jesus has given us His peace. Like the rest of the fruit of the spirit, it becomes part of our new nature when we are born again. But just like the other fruit of the spirit, we have to *yield* to peace in order for it to manifest in our lives. And, we must choose *not* to yield to anxiety and fear. It takes a conscious commitment to be obedient to God's WORD and walk in the fruit of the spirit.

In John 14:27 Jesus comforts us with these words: "Peace I leave with you, my peace I give unto you: not as the world giveth, give I unto you." Then He added: "Let not your heart be troubled, neither let it be afraid."

And in Philippians 4:6-7, the Apostle Paul said, "Be anxious for nothing, but in everything by prayer and supplication, with thanksgiving, let your requests be made known to God; and the peace of God, which surpasses all understanding, will guard your hearts and minds through Christ Jesus" *(New King James Version)*.

Notice that after Paul said, "Be anxious for nothing," he instructed us to take all our requests to God in prayer. When you pray in faith and *believe you receive* what you are praying about, then the peace of God is the result, slamming the door on anxiety. Get a visual picture that "peace...[will] garrison and mount guard over your hearts and minds in Christ Jesus," as *The Amplified Bible* says.

Peace—freedom from fear, stress, anxiety and/or depression—can be yours starting this morning. Recognize that Jesus paid the price for your peace of mind, and through The WORD of God and prayer, you can increase peace in your life, regardless of what circumstances you face!

16 *The Great Texts of the Bible, II Corinthians and Galatians,* Ed. James Hastings (New York: Charles Scribner's Sons, 1913) p. 402.

Morning
Reflection

What does (or would) peace look like in your life? How would it affect you—spirit, soul and body?

_____

_____

_____

Does having peace mean that you will never face trouble? Explain.

_____

_____

_____

How can you grow in peace?

_____

_____

_____

Today's
Connection Points

⊙ *Selections From Peaceful Praise* CD: "He Is Our Peace" (Track 7)

As you worship and praise The LORD this morning, thank Him that because you abide in Him, and He abides in you, His peace goes with you wherever you go!

⊙ DVD: "Jesus Is Your Security" (Chapter 7)

The world's system is falling apart, but God's kingdom is the place to be. Security, strength and peace are the pillars of His kingdom.

⊙ Scriptures CD (Track 7)

Philippians 4:6-7, _New King James Version;_ Psalm 3; Luke 12:25-26, _The Amplified Bible;_ John 14:27; Ephesians 3:20-21, _The Amplified Bible;_ Philippians 4:8; Isaiah 54:11-17; 2 Corinthians 4:18, _New International Version;_ Hebrews 13:5, _The Amplified Bible_

Faith in Action

Begin lifting your prayer needs, in faith, to The LORD every day, thanking Him for working "exceedingly abundantly above all that [you] ask or think" (Ephesians 3:20).
Make sure to record how He answers your prayers.

Put It Into Practice

Truthful Meditation

> I will meditate on Your precepts, and contemplate Your ways.
> —Psalm 119:15, *New King James Version*

When you mention the word *meditation* to many believers, the image that comes to mind is often a New Age interpretation. But actually, godly meditation is pleasing and right, and if you'll make it part of your life, you'll gain even deeper understanding of The WORD of God and The LORD's ways.

According to Webster's dictionary, to *meditate* is "to focus one's thoughts on: reflect on or ponder over." It requires you to slow down, get quiet and prayerfully consider a scripture or truth from The WORD. For instance, if you were to meditate on God's love for you, you would begin by asking the Holy Spirit to reveal that truth to you. You might sit quietly in your prayer time, thinking about God's love. During that time, you might reflect on the times when you've experienced God's love. You then might study scriptures that speak of His love, maybe even slowly and thoughtfully studying them, one at a time. Or you may choose to study the word *love* in Greek, Hebrew and Aramaic. This contemplative process may last for a day, a week, a month or longer. Over time, meditation like this will help you receive revelation and even begin to be more aware of God's work around you.

You can also take this same approach with a particular scripture. You could read it, prayerfully contemplate its meaning and even use a concordance to look up each word in the verse. Eventually, the Holy Spirit will begin to reveal the depth of that scripture's meaning to you.

For the purpose of this study, consider meditating on your weekly Faith in Action scriptures or one, if not all, of the following scriptures:

- "Finally, brethren, whatsoever things are true, whatsoever things are honest, whatsoever things are just, whatsoever things are pure, whatsoever things are lovely, whatsoever things are of good report; if there be any virtue, and if there be any praise, think on these things" (Philippians 4:8).
- "Thou wilt keep him in perfect peace, whose mind is stayed on thee: because he trusteth in thee" (Isaiah 26:3).
- "For God hath not given us the spirit of fear; but of power, and of love, and of a sound mind" (2 Timothy 1:7).
- "Be anxious for nothing, but in everything by prayer and supplication, with thanksgiving, let your requests be made known to God; and the peace of God, which surpasses all understanding, will guard your hearts and minds through Christ Jesus" (Philippians 4:6-7, *New King James Version*).
- "But he was wounded for our transgressions, he was bruised for our iniquities: the chastisement of our peace was upon him; and with his stripes we are healed" (Isaiah 53:5).

Let the Holy Spirit seal the truth of these scriptures in your heart and change how you approach your walk with The LORD and your life so that you can reflect His goodness and mercy in all you do!

Notes:

Fight the Temptation to Worry
by Gloria Copeland

As I shared this morning, God is trustworthy. That's a point I want to drive home to you in this Evening Connection. God wants good things for you, and He will care for you and the things that matter to you. God wants you to trust Him for everything you need. Look at Psalm 31:19: "Oh how great is thy goodness, which thou hast laid up for them that fear thee; which thou hast wrought for them that trust in thee before the sons of men!" That scripture is clear that when you trust Him, you can receive the good things He has laid up for you.

Now, I know any of us can be tempted to worry when adverse circumstances are screaming in our ears and staring us in the face. That's the time to choose 2 Corinthians 4:18: "We look not at the things which are seen, but at the things which are not seen: for the things which are seen are temporal; but the things which are not seen are eternal."

Instead of worrying, remind yourself that, as a believer, your life is no longer limited to what is common to man. People all around you may be worrying and looking for natural solutions to their problems. But, you and I depend on our heavenly Father instead of the beggarly elements of this world.

We are not subject to the "facts"—the circumstances or what the devil tries to bring. We are only subject to God and the truth of His WORD. James 4:7 in *The Amplified Bible* says, "Be subject to God. Resist the devil [stand firm against him], and he will flee from you."

Therefore, believers should not be worried about anything. *The Amplified Bible* puts it very plainly: "Do not fret or have any anxiety about anything, but in every circumstance and in everything, by prayer and petition…with thanksgiving, continue to make your wants known to God" (Philippians 4:6).

Instead of worrying, start "casting the whole of your care [all your anxieties, all your worries, all your concerns, once and for all] on Him, for He cares for you affectionately and cares about you watchfully" (1 Peter 5:7, *The Amplified Bible*).

Casting your cares on God is an act of faith. It may not be easy at first, but it is necessary if you want to live in victory.

Whether we like it or not, we're in a war—but God has equipped us to win. We can't be overcome if we follow the orders in Ephesians 6 and use all the equipment He has given us:

Be strong in The LORD, and in the power of his might. Put on the whole armour of God, that ye may be able to stand against the wiles of the devil. For we wrestle not against flesh and blood, but against principalities, against powers, against the rulers of the darkness of this world, against spiritual wickedness in high places. Wherefore take unto you the whole armour of God, that ye may be able to withstand in the evil day…. Above all, taking the shield of faith, wherewith ye shall be able to quench all the fiery darts of the wicked. And take the helmet of salvation, and the sword of the Spirit, which is The WORD of God (verses 10-17).

Lift up what *The Amplified Bible* calls "the [covering] shield of saving faith, upon which you can quench all the flaming missiles of the wicked [one]." Those flaming missiles include worry. Let the powerful sword of the Spirit fight your battle—keep The WORD going in your eyes, in your ears and coming out of your mouth.

The result will be what Isaiah 26:3 says: "Thou [God] wilt keep him in perfect peace, whose mind is stayed on thee…." Jesus confirmed that when He said, "Peace I leave with you, my peace I give unto you: not as the world giveth, give I unto you. Let not your heart be troubled, neither let it be afraid" (John 14:27).

Don't believe the circumstances or what the devil says. Replace worrying with believing what The WORD says. Make The WORD the center of your life, and it will keep you in peace.

That's what I have done all these years, and I hardly ever have a worried thought anymore. I walk in the peace that passes understanding. It doesn't make sense to the natural mind, but I'm not living a natural life!

I don't worry because I believe God's WORD. When a concern or a worry tries to come at me, I have a scripture waiting for it, ready to rebuke it. I tell that worry, "I don't believe you. I believe God. I believe if God cares for the birds, He cares for me." I don't have to figure out how He's going to do it.

When worrisome or anxious thoughts come to mind, begin taking a stand against them. Find scriptures (or use the ones I've given you in this Evening Connection) to cast those thoughts down and speak peace into your situation. Then you can enjoy peace, regardless of the situations you face.

Evening  Reflection

How do you replace worry with The WORD?

_____

_____

_____

What does it mean to say believers are not subject to facts but only to what God's WORD says? Why is this important?

_____

_____

_____

How will you respond when anxiety, stress and/or depression tempt you? Be specific.

_____

_____

_____

Today's  Prayer of Faith

I thank You, Father, I am not subject to the challenges of life, but only to Your WORD. When anxious or worried thoughts come to my mind, I ask that Your Holy Spirit bring them to my attention so I can gain the victory with Your WORD. In Jesus' Name. Amen.

Real-Life Testimonies
to Help Build Your Faith

Immediate Breakthrough!

Thank you for your prayers when I called, at the end of my tether, regarding my husband's depression. God gave us the much-needed breakthrough that very day and is in the process of healing and restoration. Thank you!

A.T.
Gloucestershire, England

Notes:

Chapter Eight

Singing the Blues:
The Deadly Nature of Grief and Depression

No More Blues!
by Kenneth Copeland

Singing the blues. It's one of humanity's favorite pastimes. Everyone does it in one form or another. Drunks balance on bar stools and blubber about how hard life is. Christians clutch their hymnals and sing mournfully about the same thing.

They all think they're doing it because they're sad. But they're not. They're doing it because, in a peculiar kind of way, they like it.

I first realized this years ago, before I met Jesus, when I was singing in nightclubs and bars. It seemed that no matter where I went, some guy would come stumbling up to me and ask me to sing *"Melancholy Baby"*—not so he could forget about his sorrows, but so he could burrow more deeply into them. So he could really, *really* get into the blues.

On the surface, that may seem strange. But, the truth is, you've probably done the same kind of thing yourself. We all have.

Why would we actually choose to feel sorrow? Because sorrow has an emotional kick to it. It offers a surge of feeling that, in the beginning stages, is almost intoxicating.

Years ago, God started jerking the wraps off grief and sorrow and unveiling their true nature to me in a startling way. He showed me that they're not the innocent emotions we've thought they were. They are actually spirit beings sent by the devil himself to steal, kill and destroy.

In fact, grief and sorrow were part of the devastating, satanic barrage Jesus took on Himself when He died on the cross. Look again at Isaiah 53:4, which says: "Surely he hath borne our griefs, and carried our sorrows." That phrase, "griefs and sorrows," can also be translated "sickness, weakness and pain." But any way you translate it, they're all pieces of the same destructive puzzle.

Grief and sorrow are part of the devil's game. They are the ever-present, shadowing companions of death. Jesus bore them on the cross, so we wouldn't have to. Yet, countless Christians are still shouldering them today. In doing so, they're ignoring the direct command in 1 Thessalonians 4:13-14, where we are clearly told to *"sorrow not"*!

Let's read that scripture: "I would not have you to be ignorant, brethren, concerning them which are asleep, that ye sorrow not, even as others which have no hope. For if we believe that Jesus died and rose again...."

Stop there and notice that according to those verses, sorrow is only for those who have no hope, who don't believe that Jesus died and rose again.

So, obviously, it's not for you! As a believer, you *do* have hope—not just where physical death is concerned but in every other circumstance, as well. In order to partake of sorrow about a particular situation, you're going to have to reject the hope you've been given through Calvary concerning that situation. You can't have hope and sorrow at the same time!

"But, Brother Copeland," you may say, "aren't grief and sorrow just natural emotions?"

Yes, they are. That's what makes them so dangerous. We've seen them as such a natural part of life that we haven't even questioned them. As believers, we've just opened the church door and let them come right in.

Webster defines *grief* as "a heavy emotional weight resulting from loss." That's how it feels, doesn't it? Like a heavy weight on your heart that's aching for release. When you give in to it, there's a rush, a wavet of emotion that rolls over you and the tears overflow. It feels good. Your friends nod, pat your back and say, "Go ahead...just let it all out." So you do, and the pressure lets up for a while, but after all the mourners and the back patters have gone home, that grief comes rising up in you again.

As a believer, you've been redeemed from the curse of grief and sorrow by the blood of Jesus Christ. You don't have to put up with them any more than you have to put up with sin, sickness or disease. So, if you'll follow the instructions in James 4:7 and resist them, they'll have to flee from you!

Psalm 107:2 tells you how to do that. It says, "Let the redeemed of The LORD *say so*".... That means when sorrow and grief start bearing down on you, say, "Oh, no you don't! I'm the redeemed of The LORD. I've been delivered from the likes of you. You just get right on out of here!"

So don't give in to it anymore. When the devil tries to burden you with grief and sorrow, resist him. You may have to walk the floor all night long. But instead of worrying and crying, walk the floor and quote The WORD until that sorry spirit leaves and the real rush and overflow comes—the joy of The LORD, which is your strength.

Remember who you are! You're the one who shall obtain gladness and joy. You're the one sorrow and grief shall flee away from. You've got no business singing the blues. You're the redeemed of The LORD. Don't you think it's about time you started saying so?

Morning
Reflection

Can you identify how grief and sorrow may have become a part of your life?

_____

_____

_____

When you give in to grief and sorrow, how does it make you feel? Does giving in to them by crying or being sad make you feel better temporarily? Does the pain then seem to quickly return?

_____

_____

_____

How should you combat grief and sorrow from now on?

_____

_____

_____

Today's
Connection Points

- **Selections From Peaceful Praise CD: "Where the Spirit of The LORD Is" (Track 8)**

  As you yield yourself to the Holy Spirit this morning, allow the peace, comfort and rest found only in Him to flow in and through you to bless and empower your day.

- **DVD: "The Joy of The LORD Is Your Strength" (Chapter 8)**

  Live long and finish strong. Reach out and grasp the joy that belongs to you through overcoming faith and trust in Him.

- **Scriptures CD (Track 8)**

  Psalm 103:1-5; Joshua 1:9; Psalm 43:5, _The Amplified Bible;_ 1 Thessalonians 4:13-14; Galatians 3:13-14; 2 Corinthians 4:13, _The Amplified Bible;_ 1 John 4:4; Colossians 3:12-17, _New Living Translation_

Faith in Action

When grief and sorrow come against you, stand in faith and say, "Oh, no you don't! I'm the redeemed of The LORD. I've been delivered from grief and sorrow. By the blood of Jesus, I'm free. So, grief and sorrow, you get out of my life!"

Put It Into Practice

Writing to The LORD

Have you ever thought to yourself, *I've got to write that down; I don't want to forget it?* Have you ever found that by writing it down, you could stop thinking about it because you knew you wouldn't forget? That's the same benefit you enjoy when you journal. Journaling is an ideal way of putting your thoughts, prayers and praise reports on paper.

If you've never done it, you may question its importance. But science supports the benefits of journaling. Researchers have found it to be a practical way of relieving stress, thinking through difficult situations and solving problems.[17]

Of course, faith-filled journaling isn't about complaining on paper. It's a spiritual exercise that reminds you of God's faithfulness. In fact, it is a lot like prayer.

1. Begin with praise and thanksgiving. Thank God for the good things in your life—your salvation, your family, your health, your home, your job, etc.

2. Write your prayer requests. The WORD says to make your requests known to God, and that's exactly what you're doing. Write about the areas in which you need assistance. Do you need a stronger relationship with your spouse? Do you need wisdom for your children or your job? Do you need financial help?

3. Record what you're learning through The WORD and your time of meditation. (See chapter 7.)

4. Listen to and follow the Spirit. As the Holy Spirit begins to reveal truth to your spirit, write it down. Let the words flow freely. Don't be concerned about spelling or punctuation. Then go back after the fact and read what you've written. Often, The LORD will speak to you and direct you through this exchange.

17 "The Health Benefits of Journaling," Maud Purcell, LCSW, CEAP, *Psych Central,* http://psychcentral.com/lib/the-health-benefits-of-journaling/000721, (2/9/2015).

Journaling can occur on any medium you choose. You may choose to write in a beautiful journal or a spiral-bound notebook. Or you may use your computer, iPad, phone or tablet. Simply choose whichever is most convenient for you.

Begin this week as you work through this LifeLine Kit. Start practicing journaling, and reap the benefits of this rewarding exercise.

Notes:

Kicking Depression Once and for All
by Gloria Copeland

In this Evening Connection, I want to continue teaching you how to be free from depression. Several months ago, one of the major news networks reported that according to their polls, six out of 10 Americans are suffering from depression. Some people would say that's understandable. It's to be expected in times like these.

But I want you to know something today. If you've made Jesus Christ The LORD of your life, depression is not normal for you. It's *not* to be expected.

You've been redeemed from it.

Just as surely as you've been made free from sin, sickness, poverty and defeat, you have also been freed from depression. Jesus paid the price for you on the cross so you could be at peace (that means "whole, complete, with nothing missing, nothing broken"), spirit, soul and body. While we've talked about this verse before in this LifeLine Kit, I want to read it again. Isaiah 53:4-5 says:

> Surely He has borne our griefs (sicknesses, weaknesses, and distresses) and carried our sorrows and pains.... He was wounded for our transgressions, He was bruised for our guilt and iniquities; the chastisement [needful to obtain] peace and well-being for us was upon Him, and with the stripes [that wounded] Him we are healed and made whole *(The Amplified Bible)*.

The New Testament confirms that. It says in Galatians 3:13 that "Christ hath redeemed us from the curse of the law, being made a curse for us." Depression is a part of the curse (read Deuteronomy 28:65-67). But, glory to God, because of what Jesus did for us on the cross, you and I have been redeemed from it!

I'll be straight, with you, though. If you don't take a stand against it, especially in these times, the devil will push depression on you anyway. He'll put pressure on your mind. He'll bring negative thoughts to you. He'll tempt you to say those negative thoughts out loud. If you yield to him, you will end up with a spirit of depression on you that will rob you of your joy, steal your health and strip you of your productivity for the kingdom of God.

Maybe that's already happened to you. If it has, there *is* a way out. It is the way of faith. Faith always overcomes anxiety and depression. If you will begin to cultivate the spirit of faith, depression will lose its grip on you.

Second Corinthians 4:13 describes it this way: "Yet we have the same spirit of faith as he had who wrote, I have believed, and therefore have I spoken. We too believe, and therefore we speak" *(The Amplified Bible)*.

The spirit of faith believes what is written in The WORD of God. It believes what God says more than it believes external evidence to the contrary. If you want to develop the spirit of faith, that's what you must do. For example, when you see in Psalm 103 that God "crowneth thee with lovingkindness and tender mercies," you must agree with that verse. Choose to believe it. Use The WORD of God to change how you think—about God, about your surroundings and even about yourself. Don't think of yourself as mistreated or pitiful. Think about yourself in God. Meditate on the fact that the Almighty God dwells on the inside of you.

Maybe all your life you've heard things like, "You're never going to amount to anything. You're not smart. You're a failure." Maybe those thoughts go around in your head like a broken record.

If that's the case, make a new record! Start spending every moment you can, reading, studying and meditating on The WORD of God. Listen to audio resources that help stir your faith. Pray The WORD, and fellowship with the Father over it. Get so full of what He says that you don't hear that old talk in your mind anymore.

Instead, you hear and speak "God talk."

God talk says, "Greater is He that is in me than he that is in the world." How can you be pitiful with the Greater One living in you? God talk says, "I'm crowned with lovingkindness and tender mercies. I'm healed. I'm prosperous. I have abundant life. God has a good plan for me. He has a good path for me, and as I seek Him, He is showing me the next step."

Don't go around saying, "I'm sick. I'm depressed. I'm confused. I'm worried." Instead, say good things about God and what He is doing for you. If you'll do that, depression will have to leave you. If you really want to get it out in a hurry, do what that last verse we read says to do. Start to sing about the goodness of God. Just open your mouth and sing a happy, grateful song right out of your spirit. Sing about how faithful God is. Sing about how much He's blessed you. Sing about how happy you are.

Make up your mind to do it. Then, by the grace of God, open your mouth and speak The WORD. Sing The WORD. Declare The WORD until you are fully persuaded that what God has promised, He is able also to perform!

Evening
Reflection

How do the words you speak affect your state of mind?

_____

_____

_____

How can you change the negative thoughts that run through your mind?

_____

_____

_____

Write three to five things you can repeat to yourself, based on The WORD, that will combat the negative things that go through your mind.

_____

_____

_____

Today's
Prayer of Faith

LORD, I commit my thoughts and my words to You. Help me to think and speak good things about myself and about my life. Holy Spirit, please bring it to my attention when my thoughts or my words reflect anything but Your faithfulness and goodness. In Jesus' Name. Amen.

Real-Life Testimonies
to Help Build Your Faith

God Brought Me Through

About a year ago I lost a good friend, a dear nephew and my closest brother all within about three months, plus my marriage was about gone from an attack of the enemy. I went through a deep depression, but I reached out to God with all that was in me. I called your prayer line, and the scriptures the lady gave me and the prayer we prayed, really gave me hope and strength. Through The WORD of God, my confession and prayer, God brought me through.

Now, a year later, my marriage is strong, I have come out of the pit of depression, and I want to thank God and your ministry for being part of my emotional healing and the healing of my marriage. Praise God for His goodness!

S.S.
Arkansas

Notes:

Chapter Nine
Guarding Your Heart

Perfect Love
by Kenneth Copeland

As we begin today's Morning Connection, let me share a powerful verse: "There is no fear in love; but perfect love casteth out fear: because fear hath torment. He that feareth is not made perfect in love" (1 John 4:18).

That verse is clear: Perfected love will get rid of fear. And, as we've already discussed throughout this LifeLine Kit, when you get rid of fear, you get rid of stress, anxiety and/or depression because, as we've already learned, fear is the *root* of all of them. When you realize you are walking in the commandment of God, there is nothing to fear. It has no authority over you.

As God's beloved, anointed children, it's amazing that we have not taken greater advantage of our authority and security that lies in the love of God. Instead, through our ignorance and man-made, religious doctrines, we've allowed the devil to oppress us and keep us in all kinds of bondage. All because of fear.

You may be wondering what possible connection there is between God's love for you and having no fear, and consequently no stress, anxiety and/or depression. That connection is found in 1 John 4:

> Whosoever shall confess that Jesus is the Son of God, God dwelleth in him, and he in God. And we have known and believed the love that God hath to us. God is love; and he that dwelleth in love dwelleth in God, and God in him. Herein is our love made perfect, that we may have boldness in the day of judgment: because as he is, so are we in this world. There is no fear in love; but perfect love casteth out fear..." (verses 15-18).

God is Love. And *in* love, there is no fear. Not an ounce.

What's more, that love—which leaves no room for fear—dwells in us. So, neither should there be any fear in us. After all, we've not been given a spirit of fear, "but of power, and of love..." (2 Timothy 1:7).

For fear to enter the heart of a believer, it must come from the outside, from the fear-infested world in which we live. And that's where *knowing* and *believing* the love of God comes into play for us.

Just moments before Jesus went to the cross, He prayed specifically for us:

> That they may be made perfect in one; and that the world may know that thou hast sent me, and hast loved them, as thou hast loved me.... And I have declared unto

them thy name, and will declare it: that the love wherewith thou hast loved me may be in them, and I in them (John 17:23, 26).

The reason Jesus gave up His place in glory, came to earth, took on the limitations of human flesh, then went to the cross, suffered and died, was so He could make that transaction.

God loves us with the same love with which He loves Jesus. And if He loves us to that degree, then He will certainly protect us to that degree. But we have to know and believe His love.

You knew the love of God the moment you were born again. It was, in fact, love that re-created you. It was love that delivered you from the power of darkness, and translated you into the kingdom of His dear Son or "the Son of His love" as it is literally translated (Colossians 1:13, *The Amplified Bible*).

But how well do you know that love?

"Well, I know God loves me, Brother Copeland. But I wouldn't go so far as to say He loves me just like He loves Jesus."

Then, you're not walking in His love by faith. You're falling back on what your flesh—and probably the devil—is telling you.

The times you don't *feel* God's presence or *feel* God's love, are the very times you had better *believe* He's there and *believe* His love for you. Otherwise, your flesh will let you down. Your mind will let you down. And, Satan will use everything he can to pressure and push you away from the love of God.

I don't care how "spiritually dry" you might *feel*. That doesn't change a thing. The WORD says the same thing today as it said yesterday. And it says, "In the beginning was The WORD, and The WORD was with God, and The WORD was God" (John 1:1).

The WORD is God. And God is Love. So The WORD is Love.

Get up every day determined to let only The WORD—Love—tell you what you feel—not your flesh, not your circumstances and certainly not the devil. Listen to Love tell you, "I will never leave thee, nor forsake thee" (Hebrews 13:5).

Remember, when we have known and believed the love of God, *"Herein is our love made perfect…"* (1 John 4:17).

Morning
Reflection

Can perfect love and fear coexist? Explain.

_____

_____

_____

Explain the verse, "God is love" (1 John 4:8). What does that scripture mean to you, and how has God's love affected your life?

_____

_____

_____

How can understanding God's love affect the way you handle fear, stress, anxiety and/or depression?

_____

_____

_____

_____

Today's
Connection Points

⊙ _Selections From Peaceful Praise_ **CD: "Near to the Heart of God" (Track 9)**

There is a place of quiet rest as you draw into the wonderful presence of your heavenly Father. He has promised to never leave you nor forsake you, and nothing can separate you from His unfailing love.

⊙ **DVD: "The Love of God Casts Out Fear" (Chapter 9)**

Love-filled faith casts out fear. Power, love and a sound mind is yours as a covenant child of your heavenly Father who loves you with an everlasting love.

⊙ **Scriptures CD (Track 9)**

Proverbs 4:20-23; Matthew 12:35-37; Proverbs 3:1-6, _The Amplified Bible;_ 1 Timothy 1:5, _The Amplified Bible;_ Proverbs 2:1-5; Galatians 6:7-9; Matthew 6:19-21, _The Amplified Bible;_ Mark 4:19

Faith in Action

Today, meditate on 1 John 4:15-18:

"Whosoever shall confess that Jesus is the Son of God, God dwelleth in him, and he in God. And we have known and believed the love that God hath to us. God is love; and he that dwelleth in love dwelleth in God, and God in him. Herein is our love made perfect, that we may have boldness in the day of judgment: because as he is, so are we in this world. There is no fear in love; but perfect love casteth out fear...."

Ask the Holy Spirit to reveal the depth of God's love for you and reflect on how that understanding affects your level of stress, anxiety and/or depression.

Put It Into Practice

Give to Live

Giving is an important act of faith and worship. It reflects the Father's heart. He gave so much so that you could live (John 3:16). And, when you give freely and joyfully (2 Corinthians 9:7), it communicates your trust in God to take care of you, your respect for the author and finisher of your faith, appreciation for all He has given you and faith that every good thing you have comes from Him.

Beyond that, giving is a spiritual exercise that opens the door to THE BLESSING and breakthrough in your life. Jesus talked about this when He said, "Give, and it shall be given unto you; good measure, pressed down, and shaken together, and running over, shall men give into your bosom. For with the same measure that ye mete withal it shall be measured to you again" (Luke 6:38).

Can giving make a tangible difference in your life as you take a stand against stress, anxiety and/or depression?

YES!

Consider these benefits to giving:

1. **Giving allows you to connect with causes bigger than yourself.** You might not be able to feed multitudes on your own, but by connecting with outreaches that do, you can make a big difference.
2. **Giving takes your eyes off of yourself.** When dealing with stress, anxiety

and/or depression, it's easy to become so focused on yourself, your problems and your circumstances, you can't see beyond your own door. By giving, especially giving your time, you are able to get your mind off of your problems and onto someone and something else. In fact, a national study found that those who give of their time exhibit lower levels of depression.[18]

3. **Giving gives you purpose.** Do you feel passionately about clothing the homeless, feeding the poor or caring for neglected animals? Giving allows you to learn about needs and motivates you to take action.

Don't wait to begin giving as you stand in faith for your freedom from stress, anxiety and/or depression. Whether you give money, resources or time, you can share God's love, make a difference in the lives of others and ultimately, reap benefits for yourself!

18 "The Health Benefits of Volunteering, A Review of Recent Research," Office of Research and Policy Development, Corporation for National and Community Service, Washington, D.C., April 2007, pgs. 3-4.

No Distractions, No Problem
by Gloria Copeland

Everything in your life begins in your heart. Do you believe that? Jesus said in Matthew 12:35, "A good man out of the good treasure of the heart bringeth forth good things: and an evil man out of the evil treasure bringeth forth evil things."

What you will have in your life tomorrow will be determined by what is in your heart today. If you allow your heart to be filled with the cares and anxieties of living, to be crowded with worries and thoughts of this natural world, then your future will be marked, not by the supernatural blessings of God, but by the sickness, poverty and calamity this world brings.

If, on the other hand, you fill your heart with The WORD and the voice of God, if you make living contact with Him each day and feast your heart on His promises and His presence, your future will be one of joy and prosperity, healing and health. Instead of chasing after the blessings of God, you'll find they're chasing you and overtaking you at every turn!

How do you keep your heart in such a state of divine fullness? By doing what we've talked about again and again in this LifeLine Kit, by spending time with The LORD every day and by making that time with Him your No.1 priority.

Notice I said your No. 1 priority. As precious as your family is, it is not the most important thing in your life. (Your family will benefit immensely from this commitment!) Your career is not the most important thing. Spending time with God is the most important thing, and once you realize that, you will do whatever you have to do to find that time. You'll wake up earlier in the morning or go to bed later at night. You'll change jobs if necessary. You'll cut things out of your life that steal your time away.

You'll never regret it either, because if you keep that union with The LORD as your No. 1 priority, He will take care of everything else.

"But Gloria," you might say, "that sounds so hard!"

If it were easy, everyone would be doing it. It is difficult in that it takes continual commitment, but it's easy in that it allows the Spirit of God to manifest THE BLESSING of God in your life. The Scripture says:

> Be not deceived; God is not mocked: for whatsoever a man soweth, that shall he also reap. For he that soweth to his flesh shall of the flesh reap corruption; but he that soweth to the Spirit shall of the Spirit reap life everlasting. And let

us not be weary in well doing: for in due season we shall reap, if we faint not (Galatians 6:7-9).

Some people assume that because they've spent days or even years studying The WORD of God, they will enjoy a harvest of God's blessings. But remember this, it is the choice you make today—not the choice you made yesterday or last month or last year—that will determine your tomorrow. The cares of this world, the deceitfulness of riches and the lusts of other things entering in will choke The WORD and make it unfruitful (Mark 4:19).

Am I saying you should never spend any time on natural things? Of course not. We live in natural bodies and have natural duties we must perform. There are times when it's good to relax and enjoy some recreation. God expects and desires that we enjoy life. He enjoys life and His desire for us is the same. When we put Him first, we live in joy.

The time you spend with God, however, is time spent building for eternity. Every moment spent with God further opens the door to His wonderful blessings and everlasting rewards.

You are building for eternity right now, even as you work through this LifeLine Kit. The minutes, hours and days of your life are the only blocks you have with which to build. So don't waste them. Use them wisely. Let your spirit be your guide. For in the end, it's only the time you give to God that will count!

Evening Reflection

Why is it so important to guard your time with The LORD?

_____

_____

_____

What do you gain from time spent with The LORD?

_____

_____

_____

List some of the distractions that have taken your attention from The LORD and His WORD.

_____

_____

_____

Today's
Prayer of Faith

Father, I thank You that You are my source for life and godliness. I put my focus on You and refuse to give in to the distractions of this world. In Jesus' Name. Amen.

Real-Life Testimonies
to Help Build Your Faith

A Lifestyle of Love Has Its Rewards

I have God's divine love within my heart, and I am learning to live the lifestyle of love, as you have preached. I'm learning to have the joy of The LORD and share it with others. I do not totally understand why now, but I do understand the grace of our Father.

I was told to search online for a pastoral nursing school for my B.S.N. I found a school, requested information online and hit the submit button. As my finger left the computer keyboard, the phone rang—it was the school! I was amazed because no more than a second had passed between hitting the submit button and the phone ringing. My lifelong dream became a reality in a matter of days: I am going to Bible school to receive my B.S.N. My credits from my nursing degree transfer. My surprise was not only the phone call after I hit the submit button, but what should have taken three to four weeks to be enrolled—financially and all—took six working days to complete. I am still in awe. One of the students in admissions stated, "This is Jesus working in your life."

At the age of 56, I can say our Father in heaven truly does love me. This is a lifelong dream come true and the doors blew open by the grace of our Father. Tears of joy are rolling down my cheeks as I type these words. I am so thankful that God loves us so much, He sent Jesus. Praise be and glory to God—Jesus is LORD!

Jacquelyn M.
Green Bay, Wis.

Chapter Ten

Living in Rest and Trusting God's Goodness

Practicing The WORD

by Kenneth Copeland

Throughout *Your 10-Day Spiritual Action Plan for Overcoming Stress, Anxiety and Depression* LifeLine Kit, we've studied how Jesus is the author of our faith. He is the finisher, or the developer of it (Hebrews 12:2). That means, when we purpose to exercise our faith, He is there to develop it, stretch it and cause it to grow. And, He does that by backing the words we put in our mouths from His WORD because He is the High Priest of our confession (Hebrews 3:1).

As we've also learned, when we make the decision to live a life of faith and love, the next step is to go to The WORD of God, find out what it has to say and do it. And, as Gloria and I have taught you, believing God's WORD, receiving it and acting on it develops faith.

I'm repeating these truths because as we come to the end of this LifeLine Kit, it's time to put together what you've learned in the past 10 days and make it lifestyle.

People often ask me, "Brother Copeland, how do you memorize all those scriptures you quote?"

Well, I never really set out to memorize a bunch of scriptures. I have memorized a few on purpose, but the majority of scriptures I know came from meditating on The WORD, believing it, speaking it, receiving it and acting on it—particularly when I set out to develop my faith in a certain area or situation.

When you do these things consistently, you will eventually become rooted and grounded in The WORD and find those scriptures easily coming out of your mouth in faith. And, that's when you can pray in tongues for a moment or two, and then just slip over into your spirit and start quoting Scripture. The WORD will just keep coming up and coming up. You get to that place by practicing The WORD.

Practicing the presence of God is much like practicing The WORD. When you practice the presence of God, you are practicing the act of listening to His voice. And the more you do it, the more you are able to hear His voice.

In reality, you are training your spiritual ears to hear. That's why Jesus told His disciples time after time, "He that hath ears to hear, let him hear."

Think about it. If you were invited to the White House to meet with the president of the United States, and you were told that you had only 20 minutes with him, would you go into the Oval Office jabbering away from the moment you were ushered in until the moment you were ushered out?

Hopefully not!

Well, as you begin to practice the presence of God, get up in the morning and say something like, "Oh, hallelujah! This is another day that The LORD has made, and I will rejoice and be glad in it...."

Then, don't allow your mind to take off thinking about what a hard day this is going to be, how you wish you didn't have to face the situations you know are out there, or worry about what you'll face.

No. Start your day by visiting with Him. "LORD, anything You need of me today, I am ready, willing and able. I'll go where You want me to go and do what You want me to do."

Then, shut up for a while and listen for His voice...enjoy His presence.

Practicing the presence of God, becoming perfected in the love of God, and becoming more skilled in The WORD of God—all these work together to develop our faith. They make all the difference in the world as you commit to enjoying a life free from stress, anxiety and/or depression.

It's the difference between just *being* free...and truly *living* free.

How do you practice The WORD of God?

_____

_____

_____

How do you practice the presence of God?

_____

_____

_____

What part does listening play in practicing the presence of God?

_____

_____

_____

Today's
Connection Points

⊙ *Selections From Peaceful Praise* **CD: "'Tis So Sweet to Trust in Jesus" (Track 10)**

Trusting in Jesus—The WORD made flesh—brings the rest, peace and joy to walk through every challenge in victory. He is your everlasting strength and Friend who sticks closer than a brother!

⊙ **DVD: "God's Perfect Peace" (Chapter 10)**

When you walk in His perfect peace, your victory is assured. Sorrow, grief, fear, doubt and unbelief will give way to the fountain of joy bubbling up in you.

⊙ **Scriptures CD (Track 10)**

Matthew 11:28-30; Psalm 23; James 1:17; Jeremiah 29:11, *New International Version*

Faith
in Action

Begin your day practicing The WORD of God and the presence of God.
Take time to read and study The WORD and then pray. Be sure to include a time of listening to what The LORD has to say to you. Enjoy His presence!

Put It Into
Practice

The Gift of Thanks

Throughout this LifeLine Kit, you've learned how important focus is. Whatever you focus on becomes your reality. As you've learned, if you focus on worry and disappointment, you receive stress, anxiety and/or depression. If instead, you focus on the good things of God and His WORD, the result will be happiness because gratitude brings happiness.

First Thessalonians 5:18 says, "In every thing give thanks: for this is the will of God in Christ Jesus concerning you." Notice that scripture doesn't say to give thanks *for* everything. God doesn't expect you to be thankful for the enemy's attacks, sickness or financial challenges. No, The WORD tells you to give thanks *in* everything. No matter what situation you face, you can give thanks for the good things in your life: your salvation, God's provision, your family, your health, your job—even the weather or nature.

Remaining thankful does three things:

1.   **Thankfulness keeps you optimistic.** Instead of wallowing in self-pity and fear, focus on the good things—and yes, there *are* good things in your life (Philippians 4:8)! Being thankful will help prevent stress, anxiety and/or depression.

2.   **Thankfulness reminds you of God's goodness.** You remember that God has been good and everything good you have comes from Him (James 1:17).

3.   **Thankfulness keeps you walking in a spirit of humility.** You realize that Jesus is your LORD, and your life belongs to Him. You may have a plan, but *His* plan for your life is the best plan for you (Jeremiah 29:11)! He's the author and finisher of your faith, and it's His purposes and plans that will succeed. Seek Him for His plan and follow it. Rest in His love for you. Develop a heart of thankfulness for His great love for you and the wonderful plan He has for your life!

Even now, begin to experience the difference it makes as you cultivate the habit of thanking The LORD for all the good things in your life. Continue to remain thankful and in faith as you focus on Him and His wonderful promises to you in His WORD.

Peace Is God's Will for You!
by Gloria Copeland

As we come to the end of this LifeLine Kit, I want to encourage you: You *can* have peace. Yes, there's trouble in the world, and as I've said before, without the protection of God, things are unsure in this life. But Isaiah 32:17-18 tells us: "The fruit of…righteousness will be peace; its effect will be quietness and confidence forever. My people will live in peaceful dwelling places, in secure homes, in undisturbed places of rest" *(New International Version).*

If we want to live in peace, we have to pursue righteousness—we have to follow God and obey His WORD. The reward is substantial—quietness, confidence, peaceful dwelling places, secure homes and rest!

Peace is such a powerful force that even if your circumstances are turned upside down and inside out, or you're caught right in the middle of financial uncertainty or tremendous emotional turmoil—even then—the peace of God can rise up within you and bring you a sense of well-being.

It is a blessing of God that no matter what's happening on the outside, you and I can live in peace, without stress, anxiety and/or depression. The Bible promises: "Great peace have they which love thy law [thy WORD]: and nothing shall offend them" (Psalm 119:165). Another wonderful aspect of peace is that it acts as God's signpost for guidance. When you have a question about what you should do, the Bible says to "let the peace of God rule in your hearts…" (Colossians 3:15).

I like the way *The Amplified Bible* says it: "Let the peace (soul harmony which comes) from Christ rule (act as umpire continually) in your hearts [deciding and settling with finality all questions that arise in your minds, in that peaceful state] to which as [members of Christ's] one body you were also called [to live]." You can allow God's peace to act as an umpire and settle questions in your mind.

Peace on earth—spiritual, emotional and physical peace—is possible. It's God's will for every one of His children…including *you*. There's no peace outside God and His WORD—outside of believing and trusting Him. So choose to spend time in prayer and in The WORD, and let the peace of God rule and reign in your life.

As we finish this LifeLine Kit, let me pray for you: "May God, the giver of hope, fill you with continual joy and peace because you trust in Him—so that you may have abundant hope through the power of the Holy Spirit" (Romans 15:13, *Weymouth).* In the mighty and precious Name of Jesus. Amen.

Evening
Reflection

What are the effects of righteousness?

_____

_____

_____

Psalm 119:165 says, "Great peace have they which love thy law: and nothing shall offend them." What does it mean to "love thy law"?

_____

_____

_____

What are the two things you must do in order to have real peace?

_____

_____

_____

Notes:

_____

_____

_____

_____

_____

_____

_____

_____

_____

_____

_____

_____

_____

Today's
Prayer of Faith

Dear LORD, I trust in You. Thank You for filling me with all joy and peace in believing. I rejoice in You, that You are faithful to Your WORD, so that I can be overflowing with hope and strong in faith through the Holy Spirit. I thank You for it. In Jesus' Name. Amen.

Real-Life Testimonies
to Help Build Your Faith

Safety in the Secret Place

We are Partners with KCM. Our 20-year-old son lives on the same street where the first bombings in Boston happened. He is a student at the Berklee College of Music, which is near the finish line of the Boston Marathon.

He said, "Mom, I was watching TV this morning and had the urge to turn it off and pray Psalm 91 and Psalm 112, so I did. I also pled the blood of Jesus over myself, all of my friends and family. We were about to walk down to the finish line when I thought, *Let's just go upstairs and hang out in the apartment for a while, then walk over.* As soon as we got in the apartment door the first bomb went off."

My son was shaken up, but safe and sound! "I praise You, LORD God, for Your faithful WORD, which kept our son, Your covenant child, safe in Your refuge." We are praying for all of Boston and every person affected.

Liz J.
New York

In what three areas have you experienced a decrease in stress, anxiety and/or depression from your use of all the LifeLine materials?

1. _____

_____

2. _____

_____

3. _____

_____

What are three steps you are taking right now to decrease your stress, anxiety and/or depression and increase your joy and peace?

1. _____

_____

2. _____

_____

3. _____

_____

As your stress, anxiety and/or depression have decreased, what are three ways you can encourage others in this area?

1. _____

_____

2. _____

_____

3. _____

_____

Appendix A

Prayers and Confessions

to Help You Stand Against Stress, Anxiety and/or Depression

Based on God's WORD

These can also be found on your Faith in Action Cards.

1. Psalm 91:1-3

I dwell in the secret place of the Most High and abide under the shadow of the Almighty. I say of The LORD, "You are my refuge and my fortress: my God; in You do I trust." Surely You shall deliver me from the snare of the fowler and from the perilous pestilence.

2. Romans 8:2

The law of the Spirit of life in Christ Jesus has made me free from the law of sin and death.

3. Psalm 91:3-7

The LORD delivers me, and under His wings I take refuge. His truth is my shield and buckler. I am not afraid of the terror by night; nor of the arrow that flies by day. A thousand may fall at my side, and ten thousand at my right hand; but it will not come near me!

4. John 16:33, *The Amplified Bible*

The world is full of tribulation, trials and frustration, but I take courage and am confident because Jesus has overcome the world. He has deprived it of its power to hurt me!

5. John 15:4-5

I dwell in Jesus, and Jesus dwells in me. I bear good fruit because I abide in Him. He is the Vine and I am a branch. I can do nothing without Him.

6. Proverbs 16:3, *The Amplified Bible*

I commit and trust everything I do wholly to The LORD. He causes my thoughts to become agreeable to His will, and so shall my plans be established and succeed.

7. Isaiah 26:3

My heavenly Father keeps me in perfect peace because my mind is continually on Him, and I trust in Him.

8. Isaiah 53:4-5, *The Amplified Bible*

Jesus has carried my griefs, sicknesses, weaknesses, distresses, sorrows and pains. He was wounded for my transgressions and bruised for my guilt and sins. He took my place, so I could be healed and made whole because of the stripes that wounded Him.

9. 1 John 4:18

There is no fear in love because perfected love casts out fear. I will not fear because I am made perfect in God's love.

10. Isaiah 32:17-18

The fruit of righteousness is peace. The effect of righteousness is quietness and confidence forever. I confess by faith that my home is secure, and an undisturbed place of rest.

Appendix B

Bonus Chapter:

Angelic Protection

With Angels and Love on My Side

by Kenneth Copeland

Before you finish this LifeLine Kit, there is one more thing I want to share with you. In this realm of walking in God's love, free from stress, anxiety and/or depression, there is a place of protection where God Himself is on the scene. Not only is He present, He is also very active.

When Israel walked in the covenant of God and kept the commandments, they had nothing to fear. The WORD of God says, "If thou shalt hearken diligently unto the voice of The LORD thy God, to observe and to do all his commandments which I command thee.... The LORD shall cause thine enemies that rise up against thee to be smitten before thy face: they shall come out against thee one way, and flee before thee seven ways" (Deuteronomy 28:1, 7).

Then, look at Hebrews 1:13-14: "But to which of the angels said he at any time, Sit on my right hand, until I make thine enemies thy footstool? Are they not all ministering spirits, sent forth to minister for them who shall be heirs of salvation?"

Think about that: There is an unseen force of the presence of God encompassing you. You are surrounded by an unseen army of angels—God's ministering spirits—moving with you at all times. When you are walking in love, this angelic force can work best in your behalf—to protect you and see that the full armor of God works, and that your prayer life is unhindered. When you walk in agreement with others, Jesus will be in the midst of that agreement to see that it comes to pass. *It is the force of Almighty God that will move people and change things.*

Remember, the weapons of our warfare, the tools with which we battle stress, anxiety and/or depression, are not carnal, or physical, but powerful through God to the pulling down of strongholds (2 Corinthians 10:4). Angelic powers are a part of our weaponry. They are ministering spirits *sent forth* into the earth to minister to and for the heirs of salvation.

The word *salvation* in the New Testament has more than one meaning. We use it most of the time in the context of being born again. The word *save* means "to be put in a sound condition." This is what happened when you were saved. It also means "healing" and "material and temporal deliverance from danger." We are heirs of God's deliverance, the deliverance created when He raised Jesus from the dead.

As I taught you in chapter 9, when you walk in the love of God, you are walking in the commandment of God. Psalm 103:20 says, "Bless The LORD, ye his angels, that excel in strength, that do his commandments, hearkening unto the voice of his WORD." When you speak and act on God's WORD in love, you allow the angelic spirits to work on your behalf.

So, make the decision to walk in God's love, starting right now. Walk free from fear, and consequently from stress, anxiety and/or depression, in every area of your life. Pray this prayer of dedication with me now:

Father, in the Name of Jesus, I ask You to bring to my attention any areas of fear, stress, anxiety and/or depression in my life. I make the decision now, and I refuse to act on fear or practice it in any way. I believe that Your love will flow through me, and I will handle every situation I am confronted with in the wisdom of God.

I believe and declare that because of Jesus' finished work on the cross, I am delivered from the law of sin and death. Fear, terror, stress, anxiety and/or depression have NO place in me. I keep the commandment of God's love and do those things that are pleasing in His sight.

I am surrounded and protected by the ministering angels of God. They keep me in all my ways. The love of God is made manifest in me, and I walk free from fear in every area of my life, in Jesus' Name. Amen.

Now, begin enjoying it! This is the beginning of the greatest and highest quality of life you have ever known. Faith works by love. What's more, it will never end. *Forever!*

Define the word *saved*. How does "being saved" affect your day-to-day life?

_____

_____

_____

What do ministering angels do for you?

_____

_____

_____

How does love affect your angels' ability to protect and serve you?

_____

_____

_____

Stay Ready

by Gloria Copeland

> He will give His angels [especial] charge over you to accompany and defend
> and preserve you in all your ways [of obedience and service]. They shall
> bear you up on their hands, lest you dash your foot against a stone.
> (Psalm 91:11-12, *The Amplified Bible*)

Did you know that one of the ways God carries out your deliverance and protection is through angels? You literally have angels at your service.

The Bible teaches that they're sent to serve you and keep you safe as you carry out God's will in your life. Hebrews 1:14 says, "Are not the angels all ministering spirits (servants), sent out in the service [of God for the assistance] of those who are to inherit salvation?" *(The Amplified Bible).*

The angel of The LORD encamps about those who fear God, to deliver them (Psalm 34:7). Your angels set up camp wherever you are. When you move, they move. When you go to town, they go to town. When you go to the grocery store, they go to the grocery store. When you go to war, they go to war.

In 2 Kings 6 you can find a picture of how angels operate. Elisha, the prophet of God, had received inside information from God on the strategy of enemy nations. He'd passed that information along to the king so Israel was never caught off guard in any military maneuver.

When the enemy king realized information was leaking to Israel, he assumed they had a spy in their camp. "Who is telling the king of Israel our military secrets?" he demanded.

His servant answered, "None of us, my lord O king. But that prophet Elisha knows what we say in our bedchambers" (verses 11-12).

So the enemy king and his entire army took off in pursuit of one man! They surrounded the city where Elisha was staying and "when the servant of the man of God was risen early, and gone forth, behold, an host compassed the city both with horses and chariots..." (verse 15).

Elisha's servant panicked. A whole army against the two of them looked like very bad odds. "Master, what are we going to do?" he cried.

"Fear not," Elisha told him, "for they that be with us are more than they that be with them" (verse 16).

Don't you know that servant was counting? *One, two! There are two of us and scores of them. Elisha must be losing his mind.* But Elisha wasn't looking at the natural realm. He was seeing in the spirit realm.

Elisha prayed, "LORD, open his eyes that he may see." Notice he didn't say, "LORD, protect me." He didn't need to ask for protection, he knew it was there.

"And The LORD opened the eyes of the young man; and he saw: and, behold, the mountain was full of horses and chariots of fire round about Elisha" (verse 17). The mountain was full of protection for Elisha! God had sent battalions of angels to protect him. I'm sure the extra angels had arrived before the enemy army ever got there. I say "extra" because we have angels surrounding us all the time, and those regulars can quickly be reinforced.

And, pay special attention to the answer Elisha gave his frightened servant in verse 16. His first words were, "Fear not."

What is the very first thing you and I are to do in trouble? Fear not. We've covered this throughout this LifeLine Kit, but let me say it again: If you give place to fear, you open the door to the devil. When you trust God, you open the door to Him.

Over and over in the Bible, God exhorts us not to fear. Psalm 91:5 begins, "You shall not be afraid...." When angels would appear to people, usually the first words out of their mouths were, "Fear not!" That's because fear and faith don't mix. Fear and faith cannot come out of you at the same time.

When you start saying things out of line with The WORD of God by speaking in fear instead of in faith, you bind the hands of your angels. You prevent them from do-ing their jobs. Psalm 103:20-21 tells us why: "Bless The LORD, ye his angels, that excel in strength, that do his commandments, hearkening unto the voice of his WORD. Bless ye The LORD, all ye his hosts; ye ministers of his, that do his pleasure."

Angels *hearken* to the voice of God's WORD. They respond to The WORD! So when your heart is full of faith and your mouth is saying, "A thousand may fall at my side, ten thousand at my right hand, but it will not come near me" (Psalm 91:7), they put that WORD into action and protect you.

But, when your heart is full of fear and your mouth is speaking words of unbelief, your angels can only stand by helplessly. It's not that they abandon you, it's just that they have nothing to act on.

Some people seem to think angels aren't around much anymore. But they are! They were present throughout the Old Testament—and they haven't gone on vacation since then. I could tell you story after story (Daniel and Peter, just to name two) where angels intervened to drastically alter the outcome of situations, both in the Bible and in our day, as well.

Some time ago, for example, one of our ministry employees was riding to work on his motorcycle when suddenly a big truck pulled across the road right in front of him. It happened so quickly there was nothing he could do. He didn't have time to think. He didn't have time to speak. He didn't have time to do anything.

Many times, that's how things happen. Suddenly, trouble is upon you. It doesn't tell you in advance it's coming so you'll have time to fast and pray. You have to be ready. You have to live every day believing God. You have to say continually, "The LORD is my refuge and my fortress." Because at those moments, you don't have time to say it.

That's how it was with that fellow on the motorcycle. All of a sudden there was a truck in front of him.

That's the last thing he remembered. He saw the truck and everything went blank. The next thing he knew he was walking around on the side of the road. A few yards away, his motorcycle lay underneath the truck.

A girl who was driving right behind him saw the whole thing. She said when the motorcycle slid under the truck, the man who was riding it went up in the air, did a flip and landed safely on his feet by a nearby fence. His only injury was a scratch on his arm! I can't imagine anything that could make that happen except angels. But here's the point: That fellow was ready. He didn't have time to grab his Bible and brush up on the 91st Psalm. He was already prepared.

That's how it has to be. You can't wait until the last minute and start memorizing scriptures when disaster strikes. You need to "say of The LORD" now. You need to *stay ready!*

Psalm 34:7 says, "The Angel of The LORD encamps around those who fear Him [who revere and worship Him with awe] and each of them He delivers" *(The Amplified Bible).* **Explain this verse and how it applies to you.**

_____

_____

How does faith affect the angels around you? How does fear affect them?

_____

_____

How can you stay ready for times when difficulties come?

_____

_____

_____

Prayer
of Faith

Dear LORD, thank You for Your ministering angels that surround me. Thank You, that as I give You and Your WORD first place in my life, do what Your WORD says and speak it out loud in faith, my heart will be filled with its power. I will be prepared to respond in faith to any situation that comes my way. In Jesus' Name. Amen.

Appendix C

LifeLine Prayer and Confession Guide

A Prayer of Victory

LORD, I put my trust in You and *refuse* to receive fear, stress, anxiety and/or depression. I praise You for the promises in Your WORD.

And now, you spirits of fear, stress, anxiety and/or depression, in the Name of Jesus, I bind you and cancel your assignment against me. I command you to go from me. You are rendered totally helpless. Your power over me was forever broken by Jesus' sacrifice on the cross.

I boldly declare that these spirits of fear have no dominion over me. What can mere men do to me? I am loosed and free from their grip, in the Name of Jesus.

I declare by faith that I am strong in The LORD and in the power of His might. I am strong, and I fear not, for You have already destroyed my enemy, the devil. You have given Your angels charge over me to protect and deliver me. I stand on Psalm 91:10 which says that no evil will befall me, neither shall any plague or calamity come near me or my dwelling place.

I praise You and thank You, LORD, that You only are my rock and my deliverer. You are my defense, I shall not be moved. I have *not* received a spirit of slavery leading to fear, but I have received a spirit of adoption. That's why I can cry, "Abba, Father!" I know that You deliver me from every danger.

You are my light and my salvation, so why should I be afraid? You are my fortress, protecting me from danger, so why should I tremble? Though a mighty army may surround me, my heart will not be afraid. I will remain confident. For You, LORD, are with me always. Your angels surround and deliver me. I am protected, in the Name of Jesus! Amen!

References: Psalm 56:3-4; Matthew 18:18; Luke 10:19; 2 Timothy 1:7; Ephesians 6:10; Isaiah 35:4; 1 Peter 5:8; Psalms 91:1, 10, 62:6; Romans 8:15; 2 Timothy 4:18; Psalms 27:1, 18:2, 27:3; Hebrews 13:15; Psalm 34:7

When You're Tempted to Worry

Father, according to Your WORD, I am anxious for nothing. I pray with thanksgiving about everything, making my requests known to You. And Your peace, which passes all understanding, keeps and guards my heart and mind through Jesus Christ.

Thank You that You keep me in perfect peace when my mind is fixed on You—because I trust in You. I seek peace, and I pursue it. Thank You that Your peace rules in my heart, and that You make even my enemies to be at peace with me!

Worry and anxiety, I resist you, in the Name of Jesus. I take authority over you. You're not the will of God for my life. I enforce The WORD of God on you. I'll not tolerate you in my life. Leave my presence, now! I am delivered from worry, anxiety and fear. Jesus bore my weakness, stress and anxiety, and I'm free. Worry and anxiety shall no longer lord it over me. Sin shall no longer lord it over me. Fear shall no longer lord it over me. Jesus has redeemed me from the curse of the law, and I proclaim my freedom, in Jesus' Name. I am loosed from your grip. Today, the gospel is the power of God unto my salvation, healing and deliverance. I receive that gospel—the good news—that I am free. I am loosed from you! I choose to believe God's WORD about my circumstances, and to walk in His peace.

LORD, I receive Your peace. Thank You that Your peace is not as the world gives. I'll not let my heart be troubled or afraid, but I'll trust in You and lean not to my own understanding of circumstances around me. In Jesus' Name. Amen!

References: Philippians 4:6-7; Isaiah 26:3; Psalm 34:14; Colossians 3:15; Proverbs 16:7; James 4:7; Luke 10:19; 2 Timothy 4:18; Isaiah 53:4; Romans 6:14; Galatians 3:13; Romans 1:16; Matthew 18:18; Joshua 24:15; John 14:27; Proverbs 3:5

A Prayer to Stop Stress

LORD, when I'm stressed and heavy-laden, I come to You, and You give me rest. You show me how to truly rest. Thank You for greater revelation of Your grace, and that You're teaching me to walk in greater and greater freedom and light that's only found in You. I cast all my burdens and cares on You, LORD, knowing that You care for me and sustain me. I refuse to fret or worry or have anxiety about anything. Thank You for helping me to rest in You and wait expectantly in faith for the answers to manifest.

Stress, I break your power off my life! I resist you in the Name of Jesus. You are not the will of God for me. I enforce The WORD of God on you. I'll not tolerate you in my life. Leave my presence. I'll never allow you back. Stress shall not lord it over me. The chastisement of my peace was upon Jesus. His peace is mine. My days of stress are over. I am the redeemed. I command every symptom of stress to leave my body, in Jesus' Name. Glory to God! I praise and thank and worship You, LORD, for delivering me from stress and anxiety, in the Name of Jesus!

And now, LORD, I choose to rejoice and fix my eyes on You, to smile, think about, and be thankful and praise You for what You have already done for me and are about to do. Thank You for Your amazing goodness and kindness in my life. In Jesus' Name. Amen!

References: Matthew 11:28-30; Psalms 55:22, 37:7; Mark 16:17; James 4:7; Romans 6:14; Isaiah 53:5; Psalms 107:2, 42:11; 1 Peter 5:7; 2 Samuel 22:7

Deliverance From Depression

LORD, I choose to walk in a spirit of praise and thanksgiving that will *always* defeat any spirit of depression that would try to oppress and afflict me. You are my refuge in time of trouble. Though my soul may be disquieted within me, I put my hope in You.

I praise You, for You are the help of my countenance. LORD, thank You that You keep me in perfect peace as my mind is stayed on You. Thank You that You have already made me completely whole, spirit, soul and body—Jesus already paid the price for my peace and wholeness on the cross. Thank You, LORD, that You never leave me nor forsake me. You are always with me. I'll not be double-minded, but I'll submit to You and resist the devil who tries to put depression on me. According to Your WORD, he has to flee from me!

Depression, you have no dominion over me! I resist you, in the Name of Jesus. I break your power off my life. You leave my presence. I'll not tolerate you in my life anymore. Jesus bore my griefs and sorrows on the cross so I wouldn't have to. So, I choose joy. The joy of The LORD is my strength! I declare that I am *strong* in The LORD and in the power of *His* might. His strength is my strength. His joy is my joy because I am His! Right now, I choose to praise and magnify The LORD. I praise You, LORD, as an act of my will, not according to my feelings. As I choose to praise You, I thank You that the enemy and the avenger is stilled and has to flee from me. Glory to God! I glorify Your Name, O LORD, and I praise You for delivering me from every evil work. Depression is an evil work. I am delivered!

Thank You, LORD, that You have not given me a spirit of fear, but of power and of love and of a *sound* mind. I cast down arguments, imaginations and resistance in my own mind to what You say in Your WORD, and I'll bring *every* thought, emotion and impulse into line with what Your WORD says. Praise God!

References: Isaiah 61:3; Psalms 9:9, 42:5; Isaiah 26:3, 53:4-5; 1 Peter 2:24; Hebrews 13:5; Romans 6:14; James 4:7; Nehemiah 8:10; Ephesians 6:10; Psalms 34:1, 8:2; 2 Timothy 4:18, 1:7; 2 Corinthians 10:5

Victory Over Anxiety

Father, I'm determined to live my life anxious for *nothing*. I pray with thanksgiving to You about everything, making my requests known to You. Your peace, which passes all understanding, keeps my heart and mind through Jesus Christ.

Thank You, LORD, that You keep me in perfect peace as I fix my mind on You. I trust in You. I seek Your peace and pursue it. I allow Your peace to rule in my heart, and I know that You will make all grace (every favor and earthly blessing) come to me in abundance, so that I may always and under all circumstances and whatever the need be self-sufficient [possessing enough to require no aid or support and furnished in abundance for every good work and charitable donation].

Anxiety and fear, I resist you, in the Name of Jesus! You have no authority over me. Jesus said I have authority over you. So, I command you by the authority given to me as a child of God, to GO from me, in the Name of Jesus! You are under my feet. I am loosed from your grip. I REFUSE TO FEAR! I believe I receive and walk in God's peace, now!

According to Your WORD, LORD, I thank You that I am like a tree planted by the water whose roots are deep, and that I won't be nervous about the heat or worried by long months of drought because I trust in You, and my hope and confidence are in You.

Thank You that Your angels surround me and my family and keep us; that no evil befalls us, neither does any plague or calamity come near our dwelling. Thank You that You are always with me, and that You never leave me nor forsake me, so that I can boldly say, "The LORD is my helper, I will not be afraid. What can man do unto me?"

References: Philippians 4:6-7; Isaiah 26:3; Psalm 34:14; 2 Corinthians 9:8, *The Amplified Bible;* James 4:7; Luke 10:19; Matthew 18:18; Mark 11:24; Jeremiah 17:7-8; Psalms 34:7, 91:10; Hebrews 13:5-6; Psalm 56:11

Stressful Family Visits/Situations

LORD, You said in the last days You would pour out Your Spirit upon all flesh. So, I thank You that You are pouring out Your Spirit on my family. Thank You that, in my family situation and relationships, what often looks like a wilderness will become a fertile field, and the fertile field will yield bountiful crops. Thank You that Your goodness and mercy brings *Your* peace into my family, and quietness and assurance forever. I praise You and thank You that my family lives in safety and quietness in their homes and all will be at rest with one another.

You said if we ask for wisdom, You give it to us generously. So I am asking for Your wisdom in dealing with my family. Your wisdom is first of all pure, peace-loving, gentle at all times, and willing to yield to others. It is full of mercy and good deeds, shows no favoritism and is always sincere. I believe I receive it, in Jesus' Name. You are the Prince of Peace, and You live in me, so I thank You that You are helping me and giving me wisdom how to plant seeds of peace and to be a peacemaker with them.

Thank You for helping me to walk in and release Your love, kindness, patience and forgiveness toward my family members by the power of Your Holy Spirit who lives in me. Let them see Your love in me, and give me opportunities to share the good news of Your love with them. Give them ears to hear, eyes to see and hearts to understand.

In the Name of Jesus, I take authority over the spirits of strife and division that would try to cause arguments and animosity in my family. I bind you and cancel your assignment against my family, according to Matthew 18:18, and I forbid you foul spirits to manifest in any way among us. I loose the spirit of unity, harmony and peace in my family. We walk in love, peace and forgiveness with each other, in Jesus' Name!

Now, I roll the care of my family members and this situation over on You, LORD, and I refuse to fret, worry or have anxiety over it. I choose to see, through the eyes of faith, my family members walking with You, living for You and fulfilling the plan of God for their lives. I rejoice, Father, because You are good, and are working in my family!

References: Joel 2:28; Acts 2:17; Isaiah 32:15-18; James 1:5, 3:17-18; Matthew 9:38, 13:15, 18:18; 1 Peter 5:7

Standing Against Fear About Your Financial Situation

Thank You, LORD, that You became poor, so that I, through Your poverty, might be made rich. You bore poverty on the Cross, so I could go free.

I believe I receive direction from You about my finances. I will be bold to give and to tithe. Thank You that as I tithe in faith, based on Your WORD, You rebuke the devourer for my sake and the windows of heaven are open to me. Thank You that You are pouring out blessings on my finances as I am obedient to Your WORD and the leading of the Holy Spirit.

You have not given me the spirit of fear, but of power and of love and of a sound mind. So, I refuse to receive the fear of lack and want, and I am confident that as I give, my gift will return to me—good measure, pressed down, shaken together and running over, poured into my lap. I trust You, LORD, and I believe You always generously provide all I need, according to Your riches in glory by Christ Jesus—with plenty left over to share with others!

I determine that no matter how my financial situation may look, I will give cheerfully, in faith, never reluctantly nor in response to pressure—for You love a cheerful giver. In Jesus' Name, I receive now, by faith, an abundant return on the seed I have sown. I do this in obedience to Your WORD.

Satan, in the Name of Jesus, I rebuke you. You are the persecutor. Take your hands off my money! I am a tither and a giver. You have no dominion over my finances. LORD, I thank You that Your ministering spirits are now free to minister on my behalf and bring in the necessary finances. I call finances into my hand, in the Name of Jesus. You come to me. I call my bills paid and my needs met!

LORD, You are the One who gives me power to be successful and get wealth, in order to establish Your covenant. I believe I receive it, now, in Jesus' Name, and I give You all the praise and glory!

References: 2 Corinthians 8:9; Malachi 3:10-11; 2 Timothy 1:7; Luke 6:38; Philippians 4:19; 2 Corinthians 9:7; Mark 11:24; Matthew 17:18; Hebrews 1:14; Deuteronomy 8:18

Standing Against Worry About a Family Member

Heavenly Father, I bring _____ before You, today, and I refuse to worry, fret or have anxiety about him/her. You promised in Acts 16:31, that if I believe in The LORD Jesus Christ, I will be saved (delivered), and my household. I'm a believer, LORD, so I thank You for the salvation and deliverance of my household.

I bind you, devil, from operating in _____'s life. I render you helpless to keep _____ out of the kingdom of God and from walking with Jesus.

Now, Father, You know who _____ will listen to. I'm asking You to send laborers across _____'s path with the anointed WORD of the living God because it's The WORD that is the powerful, incorruptible seed that brings _____ to salvation. I believe You are a place of safety for _____, and I thank You that You rescue him/her from every trap as I stay in faith for him/her. I speak protection over_____, and declare that the angels of The LORD surround _____ and deliver him/her. No evil befalls _____, neither does any plague or calamity come near _____or his/her dwelling.

Your WORD is truth, and I believe it. Therefore, in the Name of Jesus, I believe in my heart and say with my mouth that The WORD of God prevails over _____. I stand in the gap for him/her. Thank You for sending ministering angels to surround and watch over _____.

I confess that _____is a disciple taught of The LORD, obedient to Your will, and great is his/her peace and undisturbed composure! I commit _____to Your keeping, and I know and have confident trust that he/she is watched over and blessed of The LORD all the days of his/her life. In Jesus' Name. Amen.

References: Acts 16:31; Matthew 18:18, 9:38; 1 Peter 1:23; Psalms 91:3, 11-12, 34:7, 91:10; Isaiah 54:13; John 17:17; Mark 11:23; Acts 19:20; Proverbs 3:4

Overcoming Stress During the Holidays

Father, I refuse to receive stress, anxiety and/or depression of any kind, at any time! Although holiday times can add extra activities and duties to my schedule, nothing is too hard for You. And, since I am in You, I believe I receive Your supernatural help, perfect peace, anointing and supernatural wisdom to accomplish *everything* I need to accomplish, with ease, joy and time left over!

Because my body is the temple of the Holy Spirit, I take that seriously, and commit to factor in times of rest. I commit, despite any time pressure to overschedule, that I will put Your WORD first place and continue to take time to get quiet before You each day. I believe that as I *seek first* Your kingdom and righteousness, all the other things will be added to me—including time—so everything I have to do will flow with ease in Your grace. Thank You for bringing me the help I need and for supernaturally directing my steps to the right places, supplies and needed items.

I cast all my care and burdens on You, and instead of *allowing* fear, anxiety, stress and/or depression, I *choose* to keep Your praise flowing for all the good things You have already done for me this year and always! Open my eyes and ears to opportunities to bless and encourage others wherever I go, because You said it is more blessed to give than to receive. Thank You that You are always with me, and You never leave me nor forsake me.

Because You, LORD, are the source of my joy, I choose to fix my eyes on You, not the circumstances. Thank You for being so good! I set my faith for the *best* holiday time I have ever had in You. I determine that You will be glorified in my life and circumstances!

References: Jeremiah 32:17; Matthew 11:28-30; John 15:5; Psalm 28:7; 1 Corinthians 6:19-20; Psalm 37:7; Proverbs 4:20-23; Matthew 6:33; Psalms 37:23, 55:22, 42:11; Acts 20:35; Hebrews 13:5; Psalm 16:11; 1 Corinthians 10:31

When You Receive a Challenging Health Report

Isaiah 53:4-5 says that Jesus took my infirmities and bore my sicknesses, and by His stripes I am healed. And, 1 Peter 2:24 says that by His stripes I *was* healed. If Jesus already paid the price for my healing on the cross, then *I am already* healed. Jesus *took* my sickness, weaknesses and pain, so I don't have to take them. So, I declare by faith that by His stripes I have already been made whole. Therefore, I refuse to fear about this medical report! The price was paid at Calvary so I could go free.

Sickness, disease, weakness and pain, I resist you in the Name of Jesus. You are not the will of God for me. I enforce The WORD of God on you. I'll not tolerate you in my life. Leave my presence. I'll never allow you back. Sickness and disease shall not lord it over me. Jesus bore my sickness. Jesus bore my weakness and pain and by His stripes I was healed. My days of sickness and disease are over. I am the healed. I am the saved. Sickness, you leave my life. I'll not tolerate you any longer, in Jesus' Name. I receive my healing today. Right now. I command every symptom of sickness to leave my body in Jesus' Name. Glory to God!

God has not given me the spirit of fear, so I rebuke it in the Name of Jesus, and I say instead, that I have faith in God, and I am strong in The LORD and in the power of His might. No weapon formed against me shall prosper. I believe I receive my healing, and I know my prayer has great power and produces wonderful results.

My body is a temple of the Holy Spirit who lives in me, and it was given to me by God. I do not belong to myself. Jesus bought me with a high price. I'll honor Him with my body and trust Him to lead me, step by step. Thank You, LORD, that You bore my sicknesses and carried my diseases when You died on the cross. By Your stripes, I am healed. I'll keep Your words about my healing before my eyes and going into my ears daily. Your words are life to me and health to all my flesh. I will spend time daily thanking and praising You for my healing!

The price for my healing has already been paid. I plead the power of the precious blood of Jesus over my spirit, soul and body. When the devil comes against my mind with his lies about my future, I will run to God's WORD and speak His promises out loud again and again, and praise my LORD that my body is already healed, well and whole. Praise God!

References: Isaiah 53:4-5; James 4:7; Matthew 10:8; Romans 6:14; Luke 10:19; 1 Peter 2:24; 2 Timothy 1:7; Ephesians 6:10; Isaiah 54:17; Mark 11:23-24; James 5:16; 1 Corinthians 6:19-20; Psalm 37:23; Romans 8:2; Proverbs 4:23-24; Psalm 34:1; Revelation 5:9; 1 Thessalonians 5:23; 2 Corinthians 1:20

A Confession of Faith to Overcome Fear

God has not given me the spirit of fear, but of power and love and a sound mind. No weapon formed against me shall prosper, and every tongue that rises against me in judgment is condemned. Fear has no dominion over me because the Greater One lives in me. He has given me the victory in every area of life. The LORD is on my side, I will not fear. What can man do unto me? Nothing, because greater is He who is in me, than he who is in the world. The peace of God that passes all understanding guards my heart and mind through Christ Jesus.

Spirit of fear, I rebuke you, in the Name of Jesus. I cast you out of my mind. I cast you off of my body. I have no more fear. God loves me as much as He loves Jesus. The love of God is shed abroad in my heart by the Spirit of God. And love perfected casts out all fear. Fear and every bondage, you get out. Leave me now! You'll not come near my dwelling. I dwell in the secret place of the Most High God. Praise God!

I have not received a spirit of slavery to fear, but I have received the spirit of adoption whereby I cry 'Abba, Father.' I belong to The LORD, and am no longer a slave to dread, fear, stress, anxiety and/or depression. I am set free from him who had the power of death, the devil, by the precious blood of the Lamb.

I don't allow my heart to be troubled because I trust in The LORD. I stand on His promises in Psalm 91 and declare that no evil shall befall me, neither shall any plague or calamity come near me, my family or our dwelling places. The angels of The LORD surround me and watch over me and my family. I cover myself and my family with the blood of Jesus, spirit, soul and body.

Thank You, LORD, that I dwell in the shadow of Your wings, and You protect me. My steps are ordered by You, and You lead me and guide me in the way I should go. Thank You, LORD, that You are the Good Shepherd and that You watch over me and take care of me. In Jesus' Name. Amen!

References: 2 Timothy 1:7; Isaiah 54:17; 1 John 4:4; 1 Corinthians 15:57; Psalm 118:6; Romans 8:15; Matthew 10:8; John 17:23; Romans 5:5; 1 John 4:18; Philippians 4:7; Hebrews 2:14; John 14:1; Psalm 91; 1 Thessalonians 5:23; Psalm 37:23; Isaiah 48:17; John 10:14

A Confession of Faith When You're Anxious About Your Job

I am thankful, and I praise God for my job! I am grateful for and blessed with the income from my position. I choose to pay careful attention to my work, for then I will have the satisfaction of a job well-done. I have no need to compare myself with anyone else, for I am only responsible for my own conduct. I believe I receive the wisdom of God and mind of Christ to do my job with excellence. The LORD gives me His skill and wisdom to rise above my own skill level to do an exemplary job. I hear His voice in my spirit, telling me how to do things beyond my skill set.

Promotion doesn't come from the east or from the west, but it comes from The LORD. According to Proverbs 18:16 my gifts make room for me and bring me before great men and women. I hear God's voice on my job, and I know His voice, and the voice of a stranger I will not follow. I know what to do at work, and do it with confidence. I am fruitful in every good work and increasing in the knowledge of Him. Therefore, I'll not be anxious about my job, but fully confident in The LORD, who is my helper.

I'll be diligent to present myself approved to The LORD, a worker who does not need to be ashamed. According to Psalm 5:12, I am surrounded with favor as with a shield. So, I declare by faith that I have great favor in the eyes of those in authority over me in my job, and with my co-workers. I walk in God's love toward all on the job and treat them with respect. I am a blessing to my employer and to my co-workers. I'll be a vessel for honor, sanctified and useful for the Master, prepared for every good work, throwing myself into my work. He takes care of me! Amen.

References: Galatians 6:4; Colossians 1:10; Proverbs 12:24; 2 Corinthians 10:12; 1 Corinthians 1:24, 2:16; Proverbs 22:29, 18:16; John 10:2-5; Psalm 75:6; Hebrews 13:6; 2 Timothy 2:15; Psalm 5:12; Ephesians 5:2; 2 Timothy 2:21

A Confession of Faith to Overcome Depression

I choose to put on a garment of praise instead of the heavy, burdened and failing spirit of depression, so that I may be called an oak of righteousness! I set myself to constantly and at all times offer up the sacrifice of praise, which is the fruit of my lips giving thanks to and glorifying God's Name—whether I feel like it or not. I am a thankful person, and I think of others rather than focusing on myself. Depression has no place in me, and I refuse to receive it.

Depression, sadness, self-pity and oppression, I rebuke you. You are under my feet. I declare by faith that I am loosed from you, in the Name of Jesus! I break your power over my life. Jesus took my griefs. The chastisement of my peace was upon Him. I refuse to receive your torment. I choose to walk in the fruit of joy because the law of the Spirit of life in Christ Jesus has made me *free* from the law of sin and death. There is nothing too hard for God, so I choose to believe there is nothing in my life that God can't turn around.

I choose to focus on and praise God for His wonderful goodness toward me, rather than my complaints. I choose to put on a smile instead of a sad face and a frown. I choose to be a blessing to others and a cheerful encourager to those who are struggling. I choose to encourage myself in The LORD and be cheerful, for I have much to be thankful for. I fix my mind on things that are true, honest, just, pure, lovely, of good report, virtuous and deserving of praise. God's peace guards my heart and mind as I live in Christ Jesus. The joy of The LORD is my strength!

References: Isaiah 61:3; Hebrews 13:15; Ephesians 4:17; Psalm 69:30; Philippians 2:3; Luke 10:19; Matthew 18:18; Isaiah 53:4-5; Galatians 5:22-24; Romans 8:2; Jeremiah 32:17; Job 9:27; Proverbs 12:25; 1 Samuel 30:6; Psalm 107:8; Philippians 4:8, 7; Nehemiah 8:10

A Confession of Peace When Anxiety Attacks

God's peace is mine! I refuse to be anxious, stressed or fretful about anything. I bind you, Satan, from attacking my mind. I have the mind of Christ. I bind the spirit of fear, in the Name of The LORD Jesus Christ. Take your hands off of God's property. You're a liar and the father of it. Thank You, Father. I give You praise and honor. You are my LORD.

I choose to pray with thanksgiving about everything and make my requests known to You. Your peace, which passes all understanding, keeps my heart and mind through Jesus Christ.

The LORD keeps me in perfect peace, for my mind is fixed on Him because I trust in

Him. I seek peace and pursue it. God's peace rules in my heart and guards my mind. I am like a tree planted by the water, strong and tall. My roots are deep, and I am not anxious or worried about the heat or long months of drought. I trust in The LORD, and my hope and confidence are in Him.

My heart is not anxious or afraid. I trust in Him with all my heart, mind and strength, and I don't lean to my own understanding. He is my PEACE! I receive His rest.

References: John 13:27; James 4:7; Matthew 18:18; 1 Corinthians 2:16; John 8:44; Philippians 4:6-7; Isaiah 26:3; Psalm 34:14; Colossians 3:15; Psalm 1:3; Jeremiah 17:7-8; John 14:27; Proverbs 3:5; Ephesians 2:14; Matthew 11:28

Additional Materials to Help You Overcome Stress, Anxiety and/or Depression

Books

- THE BLESSING of The LORD Makes Rich and He Adds No Sorrow With It
- In Love There Is No Fear
- Know Your Enemy: Unveiling Your Real Source of Trouble
- Limitless Love
- Love Confessions
- The Power to Be Forever Free
- The Protection of Angels
- Protection Promises
- The Secret Place of God's Protection
- Turn Your Hurts Into Harvests
- The Unbeatable Spirit of Faith
- The Winning Attitude

Audio Resources

- A Lifestyle of Love
- Angels on Assignment
- Delivered From Fear…How to Live Under God's Protection
- Don't Stress Out—Trust God
- Faith in God's Love
- Freedom From Fear
- Fruit of the Spirit: Joy

- Fruit of the Spirit: Peace
- God Can Turn It Around
- God Is in Control
- In Love There Is No Fear
- Let Not Your Heart Be Troubled
- Pulling the Plug on Fear
- Seven Steps to Walking Fear Free
- Simple Stress Relief Through Thanksgiving and Praise
- The Love Factor—Living Life Without Fear
- Totally Protected

Video Resources

- A Lifestyle of Love
- Releasing God's Love in You

Digital Downloads

- Seven Steps to Walking Fear Free
- Winning Over Grief and Sorrow

Prayer for Salvation and Baptism in the Holy Spirit

Heavenly Father, I come to You in the Name of Jesus. Your Word says, "Whosoever shall call on the name of the Lord shall be saved" (Acts 2:21). I am calling on You. I pray and ask Jesus to come into my heart and be Lord over my life according to Romans 10:9-10: "If thou shalt confess with thy mouth the Lord Jesus, and shalt believe in thine heart that God hath raised him from the dead, thou shalt be saved. For with the heart man believeth unto righteousness; and with the mouth confession is made unto salvation." I do that now. I confess that Jesus is Lord, and I believe in my heart that God raised Him from the dead.

I am now reborn! I am a Christian—a child of Almighty God! I am saved! You also said in Your Word, "If ye then, being evil, know how to give good gifts unto your children: HOW MUCH MORE shall your heavenly Father give the Holy Spirit to them that ask him?" (Luke 11:13). I'm also asking You to fill me with the Holy Spirit. Holy Spirit, rise up within me as I praise God. I fully expect to speak with other tongues as You give me the utterance (Acts 2:4). In Jesus' Name. Amen!

Begin to praise God for filling you with the Holy Spirit. Speak those words and syllables you receive—not in your own language, but the language given to you by the Holy Spirit. You have to use your own voice. God will not force you to speak. Don't be concerned with how it sounds. It is a heavenly language!

Continue with the blessing God has given you and pray in the spirit every day.

You are a born-again, Spirit-filled believer. You'll never be the same!

Find a good church that boldly preaches God's Word and obeys it. Become part of a church family who will love and care for you as you love and care for them.

We need to be connected to each other. It increases our strength in God. It's God's plan for us.

Make it a habit to watch the *Believer's Voice of Victory* television broadcast and become a doer of the Word, who is blessed in his doing (James 1:22-25).

About the Authors

Kenneth and Gloria Copeland are the best-selling authors of more than 60 books. They have also co-authored numerous books including *Family Promises,* the *LifeLine* series and *From Faith to Faith—A Daily Guide to Victory.* As founders of Kenneth Copeland Ministries in Fort Worth, Texas, Kenneth and Gloria have been circling the globe with the uncompromised Word of God since 1967, preaching and teaching a lifestyle of victory for every Christian.

Their daily and Sunday *Believer's Voice of Victory* television broadcasts now air on more than 500 stations around the world, and the *Believer's Voice of Victory* magazine is distributed to nearly 600,000 believers worldwide. Kenneth Copeland Ministries' international prison ministry reaches more than 20,000 new inmates every year and receives more than 20,000 pieces of correspondence each month. Their teaching materials can also be found on the World Wide Web. With offices and staff in the United States, Canada, England, Australia, South Africa, Ukraine and Singapore, Kenneth and Gloria's teaching materials—books, magazines, audios and videos—have been translated into at least 26 languages to reach the world with the love of God.

When The LORD first spoke to Kenneth and Gloria Copeland about starting the *Believer's Voice of Victory* magazine...

He said: *This is your seed. Give it to everyone who ever responds to your ministry, and don't ever allow anyone to pay for a subscription!*

For more than 45 years, it has been the joy of Kenneth Copeland Ministries to bring the good news to believers. Readers enjoy teaching from ministers who write from lives of living contact with God, and testimonies from believers experiencing victory through God's Word in their everyday lives.

Today, the *BVOV* magazine is mailed monthly, bringing encouragement and blessing to believers around the world. Many even use it as a ministry tool, passing it on to others who desire to know Jesus and grow in their faith!

Request your FREE subscription to the *Believer's Voice of Victory* magazine today!

Go to **freevictory.com** to subscribe online, or call us at **1-800-600-7395** (U.S. only) or **+1-817-852-6000**.

We're Here for You!®

Your growth in God's WORD and your victory in Jesus are at the very center of our hearts. In every way God has equipped us, we will help you deal with the issues facing you, so you can be the **victorious overcomer** He has planned for you to be.

The mission of Kenneth Copeland Ministries is about all of us growing and going together. Our prayer is that you will take full advantage of all The LORD has given us to share with you.

Wherever you are in the world, you can watch the *Believer's Voice of Victory* broadcast on television (check your local listings), the Internet at kcm.org, or our digital Roku channel.

Our website, **kcm.org,** gives you access to every resource we've developed for your victory. And, you can find contact information for our international offices in Africa, Asia, Australia, Canada, Europe, Ukraine and our headquarters in the United States.

Each office is staffed with devoted men and women, ready to serve and pray with you. You can contact the worldwide office nearest you for assistance, and you can call us for prayer at our U.S. number, +1-817-852-6000, 24 hours every day!

We encourage you to connect with us often and let us be part of your everyday walk of faith!

Jesus Is LORD!

Kenneth & Gloria Copeland

Kenneth and Gloria Copeland